CASH FLOW
AND HOW TO
IMPROVE IT

CASH FLOW

AND HOW TO

IMPROVE IT

LEON HOPKINS

KOGAN
PAGE

First published in 1993

Apart from any fair dealing for the purposes of research or private study, or criticism or review, as permitted under the Copyright, Designs and Patents Act, 1988, this publication may only be reproduced, stored or transmitted, in any form or by any means, with the prior permission in writing of the publishers, or in the case of reprographic reproduction in accordance with the terms of licences issued by the Copyright Licensing Agency. Enquiries concerning reproduction outside those terms should be sent to the publishers at the undermentioned address:

Kogan Page Limited
120 Pentonville Road
London N1 9JN

© Leon Hopkins 1993

British Library Cataloguing in Publication Data

A CIP record for this book is available from the British Library.

ISBN 0-7494-0908-8

Typeset by Books Unlimited (Nottm) – Sutton in Ashfield, NG17 1AL
Printed and bound in Great Britain by Clays Ltd, St Ives plc

Contents

Preface

Sparkling salesmanship, meticulous manufacturing and magic marketing count for nothing unless the end result is more money coming in than going out.

Even profitable businesses go broke if they run out of cash. And the more successful they are, the greater the problems they face in finding the money needed to cover expansion.

Conversely, loss-making businesses can survive, in the shorter term at least, provided they take care to have enough ready money to pay their way.

Making the most of business opportunities means making the most of cash resources. Whether on an upward path or up against it, cash management will always be critical.

Keys to successful cash flow management are planning and information.

Planning ahead allows likely dips in the bank balance to be smoothed over and longer-term cash needs to be anticipated and catered for.

Information allows the business to keep a check on how well its plans are working out, to make adjustments along the way and, if necessary, to have breathing space for emergency action to take effect.

This book sets out to explain the relationship between profitability and cash flow, how cash needs can be managed so that they are kept to the minimum and how those needs can be anticipated and met. And in case of unforeseen problems, there is a list of possible emergency measures.

8 Cash Flow and How to Improve it

Profitability is the measure of business success. But profits are useless unless they can be translated into hard cash and used effectively.

1. Canute was wrong

King Canute may have failed to stop the tide, but in business affairs any astute manager can alter the rate at which cash flows in or out.

Cash flow is an easy enough concept. 'We're having cash flow problems', says the customer trying to put off paying his bill. He means he hasn't got enough in the bank to cover the cheque you are demanding. But the problem, he implies, will be short lived. The finances of the business are on a sound footing, it is just that there has been a temporary hitch due to some unexpectedly large bills or slow-paying customers of his own.

Of course, the business does not need to have a credit balance at the bank to emerge from its cash flow problems; it might very well always operate with an overdraft. But it must gain access to a means of making payments by ensuring it is able to operate within its overdraft limit or by agreeing an increase to that limit.

Sign of danger

It is true that 'cash flow problems' sometimes are only a blip in the bank balance. Often they are a sign of danger, of under-financing, slack management or lost opportunities.

If cash fails to flow for any length of time the very least that will happen to your customer will be a rein on the development of his business. More likely, he will gain a bad name in the trade, his credit will be reduced and the problem will get worse. In the end he will have to find additional finance or shut up shop.

Maintaining a balance

Every business has cash flowing in and cash flowing out. To survive and prosper the two must be in balance, not necessarily from day to day, but certainly over a period of any length. Like the tide, the ebb and flow erodes the financial coastline and allows the business to advance.

In comes cash from sales, from extra owners' capital and from borrowing (Figure 1.1). Out goes cash for purchases, for overheads, for dividends and owners' drawings – and for investment in new, more or better machinery, premises, cars, vans and other equipment, for research and development, to fund the launch of new products or brands, or for the purchase of designs or patents, or other businesses.

Cash flow management means smoothing out these tidal movements so they are no more than an orderly and predictable ripple that will not sink the boat.

Business performance

For tiny businesses with little need of tools and equipment, no credit sales and no VAT, there may not be much difference between day-to-day sales and purchases and the inflow, or outflow, of cash. But for businesses of any size there is a world of difference.

Business performance is measured in terms of income achieved and costs incurred, irrespective almost of when cash actually changes hands. The business takes credit for its sales when delivery is made of the goods and an invoice is raised. And to arrive at a profit it 'matches' against this income the cost of those goods sold (Figure 1.2).

Of course, the actual goods sold may well have been bought and paid for a good while before, even turned from various parts and materials into a finished product and kept in stock for months. If the goods are sold on credit, the money for them will probably not come in for at least a few weeks, perhaps longer.

Day-to-day transactions cause ever-changing fluctuations in the bank balance. More permanent changes in cash resources can occur or accumulate for a number of reasons.

Cash resources will increase as a result of:

- *Increased owners' capital* – say an issue of new shares;

- *Increased borrowing* – either long-term loans or shorter-term overdrafts, hire-purchase agreements or the like;

- *Trading profits* – the excess of trading income over trading costs;

- *Reductions in working capital* – caused by contraction of the business or improved control;

- *Sale of fixed assets* – revenue from the sale of buildings, machinery, vehicles and the like.

Cash resources will be used up by:

- *Loan repayments* – the capital element of both short- and long-term loan repayments;

- *Trading losses* – any short-term excess of trading costs over trading income;

- *Increased working capital* – caused by expansion or other planned or unplanned increases in stock or debtor levels;

- *Purchase of fixed assets* – either as replacements or as improvements or additions;

- *Owners' reward* – payment of owners' drawings or, in the case of a company, dividends;

- *Taxation* – taxation due on profits.

Figure 1.1 *Cash flow sources and uses*

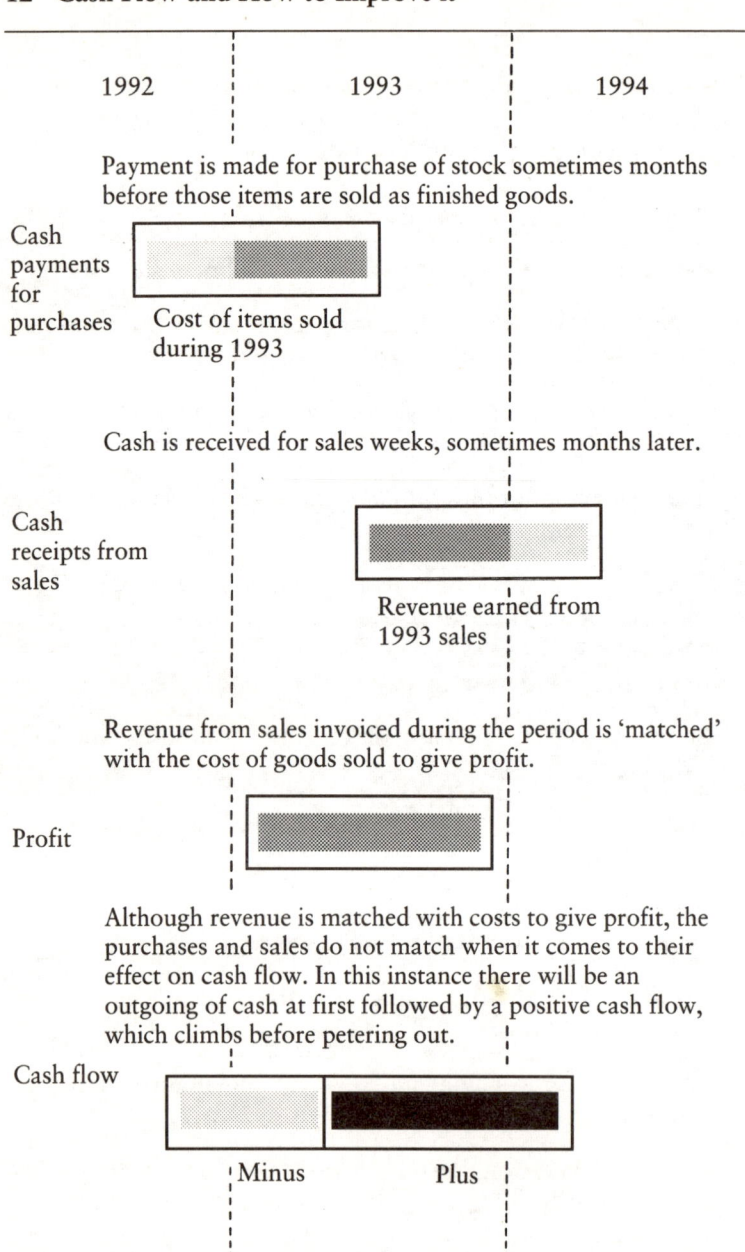

Figure 1.2 *The matching concept and cash flow*

So the 'matched' sales and purchases do not match at all when it comes to their effect on the bank statement.

Value added tax

Value added tax is another reason that profit and loss and bank statement figures will differ.

When a sale has been made by a VAT-registered business, except when the goods involved are zero rated or exempt, VAT must be added to the invoice. In turn, the business will have VAT added to any invoices received for purchases.

But there is no profit or loss on VAT. Instead, the general principle is that businesses act as agents, paying over to or claiming back from Customs and Excise the net difference between the VAT collected and VAT paid.

The accounting and cash flow consequence is that profit and loss figures, which represent net costs and net income, will exclude VAT. But cash flow, which is generated by invoices issued and received, will include VAT.

Revenue and capital

Besides VAT, some other cash coming into or going out of the business will not affect profit directly at all (Figure 1.3). A distinction is made traditionally between 'revenue' items and 'capital' items.

Revenue items, like purchases and sales, are to do with day-to-day trading – things that are bought to be *used up*, rather than *used in*, the business, and sold to make an immediate turn rather than to realise cash tied up in capital equipment.

Capital items are to do with the longer term and include, for example, long-term loans to the business or purchases or sales of premises, vehicles or plant.

If a van is purchased to be used in the business to earn profits over four years, it would be unfair to charge the whole cost against the year in which it is bought. So in calculating performance the cost

Not all costs or receipts affect profits. Some are capital items that impact mainly on the balance sheet while others can be classified as revenue but are payments out of profits rather than charges to be set against income in arriving at a pre-tax profit. Or, as in the case of VAT and PAYE, they may be wholly or entirely amounts collected by the company to be paid over to the relevant authorities.

	Revenue items	Capital items	Cash flow affected
Sales income	Yes*		Yes
Purchases of raw materials	Yes*		Yes
Purchases of goods for resale	Yes*		Yes
Wages (incl. employers PAYE and NI)	Yes*		Yes
Overheads (excl. depreciation)	Yes*		Yes
Depreciation	Yes*		No
Interest	Yes*		Yes
Taxation	Yes		Yes
Drawings/dividends	Yes		Yes
VAT/PAYE	Yes		Yes
Borrowing		Yes	Yes
Sale of fixed assets		Yes	Yes
Loan repayments		Yes	Yes
Purchase of fixed assets		Yes	Yes

Asterisked items affect the calculation of pre-tax profits. Remember that sales income and purchases will be net of VAT when it comes to calculating profit but gross of VAT in their cash flow consequences.

Depreciation is a special case. It is a notional charge against profits calculated as a proportion of the cost of fixed assets in use with reference to their expected useful life. Cash flow is affected by the purchase of fixed assets but not by the depreciation charge.

Figure 1.3   *Profit and cash flow*

is spread over the four-year working life of the van – and therefore probably in a way which has no bearing on how it is paid for.

Finally, there are payments out of and to the business which are neither trading nor capital items. These are distributions of profits to the owners of the business – dividends in the case of a company, drawings in the case of a sole trader or partnership – payments or refunds of taxation based on profits (or losses), and of the net difference between VAT collected, or due to be collected, from customers and paid to suppliers.

Managing cash flow

Cash flow, then, cuts across the accounting divide between capital and revenue. It is to do with finance, and embraces both long- and short-term borrowing, fixed capital and working capital requirements, and asset management.

Profitability, the 'bottom line', is the accepted indicator of overall business success or failure. But profitability does not guarantee a healthy bank balance. The 'bottom line' for most businesses is that to survive and prosper they must manage both profitability and cash flow.

This means managing short-term cash fluctuations caused, most frequently, by the inevitable cut and thrust of day-to-day trading, but most violently by often entirely predictable major financial events. It also means monitoring and providing for longer-term trends, such as a reduction in profitability which will inevitably lead to a drain on cash.

Financial structure

The balance sheet is a means of recording the way the finance of a business is structured. It is also a useful means of visualising how the elements of cash flow interact.

In traditional format the balance sheet has four sectors which can be thought of as building blocks (Figure 1.4).

	What is owed	What is owned or due
Long term	**A CAPITAL EMPLOYED** Owners' capital Long-term loans Accumulated profits and other reserves	**B FIXED ASSETS** Tangible assets: Land and buildings Plant and equipment Vehicles Intangible assets: Goodwill Trademarks Patents
Short term	**C CURRENT LIABILITIES** Trade creditors Accruals Taxation VAT/PAYE Overdraft	**D CURRENT ASSETS** Stock Work in progress Trade debtors Prepayments Cash at bank

The balance sheet provides a way of visualising the financial structure of the business and the relationship of cash to other assets and liabilities. It also provides a clue to how the cash position can be improved.

What is owed (A + C) will always equal what is owned or is due to the business (B + D).

Working capital is represented by current assets less current liabilities (D – C) and, if a business is to pay its way, should usually be a positive figure.

Capital employed in the business – owners' capital plus long term loans and retained profits – will always equal net assets – fixed assets plus working capital (B + D – C).

As the balance sheet must balance, cash resources can be increased by making blocks A and C larger or by shrinking block B. Within block D cash will be larger if stock, work in progress or trade debtors are made to shrink.

Figure 1.4   *Financial structure and cash flow (outline balance sheet)*

The top two blocks, A and B in Figure 1.4, represent longer-term items, and the lower two, C and D, more immediate items. The two blocks on the left, A and C, detail what is owed, and the two on the right, B and D, what is owned by or due to the business.

The top left-hand block therefore shows what the business has borrowed from its owners and others to use long term in the business – it represents the 'capital employed'.

This is used to provide plant, premises, vehicles and other fixed assets ('capital' items in the split between revenue and capital mentioned above) and working capital.

This last item represents unfinished business in the 'revenue' department and is the net of the two lower blocks representing current assets (such as stock and outstanding debtors) and current liabilities (such as outstanding bills).

Since these are amounts that are expected to be received and must be paid in the near future, it follows that to be sure of paying its way the business must usually have more current assets than current liabilities.

Improving cash resources

The balance sheet will always balance – it is an arithmetical certainty of the double entry bookkeeping methods that form the basis of all accounting, whether manual or computerised. Therefore the two left-hand blocks will always total the same as the two right-hand blocks. This gives the clue to how cash resources can be improved.

Either one or other of the two left-hand blocks must be made to grow, or the top right-hand block made to shrink.

The long-term cash position can be improved by increasing block A – by introducing more capital to the business or by improving profits; or by reducing block B – perhaps selling off some assets. The short-term position can be improved by increasing block C – by increasing creditors (the obvious solution of not paying bills) or by reducing the non-cash items within block D.

Room for manoeuvre within this current asset block includes reducing stocks and work-in-progress, perhaps by better control, or reducing debtors, say by persuading customers to pay up faster.

Each of these options will be looked at in more detail in later chapters.

Cash resources can be increased by:

- putting more capital into the business;

- borrowing;

- making profits;

- selling fixed assets;

- paying creditors more slowly;

- reducing stock levels;

- making debtors pay faster;

- better use of cash.

Figure 1.5   *Improving cash resources*

2. Planning – the key to control

Few succeed in business without a plan.

Like a ship setting sail, the business needs to set its sights on a destination, plot a course, note the shoals, reefs and other dangers along the way, and take account of the tides.

At the simplest level the plan must be to generate sufficient income to cover costs and leave something over for profit. But, in the main, business activities cannot be summed up quite so easily. The plan must take into account the cost of raw materials and of wages and overheads, the effects on sales of different levels of mark up, marketing strategy, finance and a host of other details.

It must also break down trading into useful time bites so that trends and shorter-term fluctuations can be identified.

Budgets

Typically, a business of any size might have some sort of strategic plan covering a number of years and, most importantly, shorter-term budgets setting out anticipated weekly, monthly or quarterly sales, costs and profits throughout the coming year. So, for example, a small engineering company might have budgets for sales quantities, prices to be achieved and total sales revenue for each major product line or category. It would have corresponding budgets for raw material costs and for wages – based on the level of production needed to meet expected sales and the level of overtime this would entail (Figure 2.1).

And there would be budgets for other major costs and overheads.

		Jan.	Feb.	Mar.	Total
Sales:					
Pump casings:	Quantity	12,500	25,000	13,300	50,800
	Price	£1.80	£1.20	£1.80	£1.50
	Sales value	£22,500	£30,000	£23,940	£76,440
Piston rods:	Quantity	3,600	3,200	4,000	10,800
	Price	£3.75	£3.75	£3.80	£3.77
	Sales value	£13,500	£12,000	£15,200	£40,700
		£	£	£	£
Total sales value		36,000	42,000	39,140	117,140
Manufacturing costs					
Raw materials:					
Pump cases – 50p each		6,250	12,500	6,650	25,400
Piston rods – 45p each		1,620	1,440	1,800	4,860
Total		7,870	13,940	8,450	30,260
Manufacturing wages		7,600	12,800	7,800	28,200
Manufacturing overheads		3,750	3,750	3,750	11,250
Total manufacturing costs		19,220	30,490	20,000	69,710
Margin on manufacturing		16,780	11,510	19,140	47,430
Other costs					
Sales and marketing		3,600	3,600	4,700	11,900
Distribution		3,750	4,500	3,990	12,240
Administration		2,750	2,750	2,750	8,250
Finance		1,100	1,100	1,100	3,300
Total		11,200	11,950	12,540	35,690
Trading profit		5,580	(440)	6,600	11,740

Figure 2.1   *Madeup Engineering Company: summary budget – first quarter 1993*

Depending upon the size of business and degree of budgeting sophistication, the overall budget is likely to be compiled from a series of departmental or divisional budgets, each the responsibility of a particular manager.

So it is possible the engineering company mentioned above might have two plants each producing different products and each operated as separate businesses or 'profit centres'. The manager of each would have put forward his or her own budget for expected revenue, costs, and profit (Figure 2.2). This in turn would have been compiled from a series of revenue and cost budgets.

Sales managers would be made responsible for their own sales budgets and other managers for particular 'cost centre' budgets.

Built up in this way budgets give an indication of the likely trading results for the coming months. If everything goes according to plan, the figures in the budget should be the same as those in the profit and loss account.

Not the whole story

But, as was seen in the last chapter, the profit and loss account does not tell the whole story. The profit destination may be desirable and the business course correct, but if the timing is wrong the vessel may be left high and dry by an ebb cash tide. In other words, a separate budget is needed for cash flow.

There are two principal reasons for this. The first is to ensure the business has adequate funds available at all times to meet its business plans. And the second is that the cost of finance must be calculated and written into the budget and this can only be achieved if likely current account credit balances or overdrafts are known.

Enter the cash flow statement

All business actions have cash implications, and the cash flow statement provides a means of calculating those implications in advance, and monitoring their effect after the event.

Pump plant

		Jan.	Feb.	Mar.	Total
Sales:	Quantity	12,500	25,000	13,300	50,800
	Price	£1.80	£1.20	£1.80	£1.50
	Sales value	£22,500	£30,000	£23,940	£76,440
		£	£	£	£
Raw materials:					
Pump cases – 50p each		6,250	12,500	6,650	25,400
Manufacturing wages		4,900	10,100	5,100	20,100
Manufacturing overheads		2,400	2,400	2,400	7,200
Total manufacturing costs		13,550	25,000	14,150	52,700
Margin on manufacturing		8,950	5,000	9,790	23,740

Piston-rod plant

		Jan.	Feb.	Mar.	Total
Sales:	Quantity	3,600	3,200	4,000	10,800
	Price	£3.75	£3.75	£3.80	£3.77
	Sales value	£13,500	£12,000	£15,200	£40,700
		£	£	£	£
Raw materials:					
Piston rods – 45p each		1,620	1,440	1,800	4,860
Manufacturing wages		2,700	2,700	2,700	8,100
Manufacturing overheads		1,350	1,350	1,350	4,050
Total manufacturing costs		5,670	5,490	5,850	17,010
Margin on manufacturing		7,830	6,510	9,350	23,690

Figure 2.2 *Madeup Engineering Company: manufacturing profit centre budget – first quarter 1993*

	Jan. (£)	Feb. (£)	Mar. (£)	Total (£)
Receipts: Trading – sales	36,542	43,592	46,176	126,310
Capital – sale of land			25,000	25,000
Total	36,542	43,592	71,176	151,310
Payments: Manufacturing costs: Raw materials –				
Casings	5,875	12,455	5,287	23,617
Rods	1,125	1,845	1,650	4,620
Wages (excl. PAYE)	4,900	8,600	5,100	18,600
PAYE	2,000	2,700	4,200	8,900
Overheads (excl. depreciation and rent)	2,000	1,750	2,500	6,250
Rent		5,000		5,000
Sales and marketing costs	2,500	3,600	3,600	9,700
Distribution costs	3,300	3,750	4,500	11,550
Administration costs	3,000	3,000	3,000	9,000
Finance costs – Hire-purchase interest	900	900	900	2,700
Bank interest		600		600
Other – Taxation	17,000			17,000
VAT		9,600		9,600
New car (deposit)	5,000			5,000
Hire-purchase repayments	3,000	3,000	3,000	9,000
Total	50,600	56,800	33,737	141,137
Net movement	–14,058	–13,208	37,439	10,173
Opening bank balance	19,600	5,542	–7,666	19,600
Net movement	–14,058	–13,208	37,439	10,173
Closing bank balance	5,542	–7,666	29,773	29,773

Figure 2.3 *Madeup Engineering Company: summary cash flow statement – first quarter 1993*

The statement (Figure 2.3) is a mirror image of other budget statements recording not a weekly, monthly or quarterly estimate of revenue earned nor the 'matched' costs – the figures that would appear in the profit and loss account – but the expected receipts and payments. The object is to arrive at an estimate of the bank balance likely at the end of each budgeting interval. This means that any VAT on sales or purchases must be added to the net-of-VAT figures included in the budget. It also means delaying sales revenues by the average time customers take to pay invoices and adjusting the timing of raw material costs to take account of manufacturing periods, changes in stock levels and supplier credit terms. (Remember Figure 1.2?)

And depreciation charges must be excluded – depreciation is not an actual cash payment – but the impact of receipts and payments that do not affect pre-tax profits directly must be added in. These items will include taxation, VAT settlements, PAYE deductions, borrowing and loan repayments, and sales or purchases of assets (Remember Figure 1.3?) Businesses with significant capital investment programmes should have separate capital expenditure budgets from which to draw this last information.

Preparing a cash flow statement

Just as compiling budgets is usually a matter of working from the particular to the general, a careful step-by-step process, so putting together a cash flow statement involves calculations using the same basic information. The degree of detail included and the interval frequency used will depend very much upon the size and nature of the business and possibly on the tightness of the margins within which it has to work.

While it would be pointless to produce statements in more detail than needed for accuracy and understanding, the actual calculations themselves need not be unduly cumbersome, given access to a personal computer and spreadsheet program which make the whole process relatively painless.

Sales income

By the time it comes to prepare a cash flow statement the expected sales income will already have been estimated. Filling in the anticipated bankings resulting from those sales is therefore a matter of adjusting back for the delay between issuing an invoice and actually receiving a cheque in payment and adding on the VAT.

Provided sales are not dominated by one or just a few large customers and that payment experience does not vary dramatically between different classes of customer, it will usually be quite adequate to use averages to make these adjustments. Where there are substantial differences in agreed or accepted trade terms between different classes of customer, separate cash flow calculations may have to be made for each class.

Likewise, if sales include one or more particularly large contracts on special terms, or one or just a few particularly important customers who enjoy special treatment, then again separate calculations are likely to be needed for this element of sales (Figure 2.4).

Other receipts and payments

Most other categories of income and expenditure will also require adjustment to arrive at a cash flow statement equivalent. Often the requirement is only one of putting forward the item by a month or two to reflect agreed credit terms and adding in any VAT. But some items require particular thought. These include the following:

Capital items and depreciation

Few business can operate without fixed assets of some kind – such things as cars, vans, lathes, desks, buildings. But although they are the tools for doing business, purchases and sales of fixed assets only have an indirect impact on accounting profits. This is because in accounts their cost is spread over their expected working life by means of a notional charge known as depreciation. Of course, actual payments and receipts involved in buying or selling fixed assets are far from notional. So while the profit and loss account and revenue budgets will include a depreciation charge, the cash flow statement must include the actual cash amounts paid or received.

Dividends

Dividends are the amounts paid by companies to shareholders by way of a share of profits. The actual amount and timing is entirely within the control of the company – albeit that the largest companies will have to pay heed to the effect of dividend decisions on their share price.

For smaller companies special attention needs to be given to dividends on two counts.

First, they are a distribution of profits rather than a charge against profits. Many smaller companies do not prepare budgets covering this aspect of their operations so it is important that, if a dividend is anticipated, its effect must be reflected in the cash flow statement.

Second, there is a tax consequence to incorporate in the cash flow. Companies pay dividends net of tax – shareholders receive dividends with tax at the standard rate already deducted. The amount deducted is known as Advance Corporation Tax since the company can eventually set it against any Corporation Tax due on profits. But in the mean time it must pay over the amount involved at the end of a three-month period.

Goods for resale

Goods purchased for resale will also be affected by likely changes in stock levels. Building up stocks will tend to bring forward the outflow of cash; running them down will put it back.

Hire purchase and leasing payments

Hire purchase and leasing are both means of financing the acquisition of capital items such as vehicles, office equipment or plant and machinery. The difference between the two approaches is often down to a matter of fine print but each requires a slightly

Standard trade terms for pump casings are 30 days' credit. In practice, 60 per cent of customers pay on time while the remainder hold out for 60 days.

The company has secured a major contract for the supply of 15,000 casings in February. Negotiations were tough and Madeup was knocked down to a price of just 80p per casing. However, the customer agreed to pay 50 per cent of the invoice cash on delivery with the remainder 30 days later.

Piston rods are sold to one major customer only, with payment of each invoice made on 60 days.

Regular deliveries of both products are made throughout every month so that an average mid-month invoicing date is assumed for the purposes of estimating cash flow.

	Total £	Jan. £	Feb. £	Mar. £
Expected receipts:				
Pump casings:				
November 1992 sales				
£21,000 plus VAT	24,675	9,870	—	—
December 1992 sales				
£16,500 plus VAT	19,387	11,632	7,754	—
January 1993 sales				
£22,500 plus VAT	26,437	—	15,863	10,574
February 1993 sales				
£18,000 plus VAT	21,150	—	—	12,690
February 1993 special contract				
£12,000 plus VAT	14,100	—	7,050	7,050
March 1993 sales				
£23,940 plus VAT	28,130	—	—	—
Piston rods:				
November 1992 sales				
£12,800 plus VAT	15,040	15,040	—	—
December 1992 sales				
£11,000 plus VAT	12,925	—	12,925	—
January 1993 sales				
£13,500 plus VAT	15,862	—	—	15,862
February 1993 sales				
£12,000 plus VAT	14,100	—	—	—
March 1993 sales				
£15,200 plus VAT	17,860	—	—	—
Total		36,542	43,592	46,176

Figure 2.4 *Madeup Engineering Company: sales receipts – cash flow calculation – first quarter 1993*

different accounting treatment and different adjustment when converting between revenue budgets and cash flow statements.

Hire purchase involves making a deposit, most of which may comprise the VAT element of the purchase price (which VAT-registered traders may claim as an input item in their next VAT return), plus a series of equal repayment instalments. No VAT is included in the instalments, which comprise in effect part capital repayment, part interest charge – in the same way that a monthly mortgage repayment includes both a repayment of principal and a payment of interest.

Revenue budgets should include the interest charge part of instalments only – loan repayments do not affect profits but are a capital item.

Cash flow statements should include both the interest and principal element since this is the amount flowing out of the bank statement.

Leasing arrangements also usually involve an up-front payment, but this time in the form of leasing payments in advance. All

	Hire purchase	Leasing
Deposit or advance payment required	Yes	Yes
VAT included in initial payment	On total purchase price	On advance payments only
Initial deposit/payment a charge against profits?	No	Yes
Regular instalments/payments required	Yes	Yes
VAT included in instalments/payments	No	Yes
Instalments/payments a charge against profits?	Interest element only	Yes
Depreciation charge against profits	Yes	No

Figure 2.5 *Hire purchase and leasing payments: cash flow consequences*

leasing payments must bear VAT and it is this gross amount that will appear in cash flow statements. The net amount, excluding VAT, is the amount which will be charged against profits and will therefore appear in budget statements (Figure 2.5).

Raw materials

In manufacturing businesses the pattern of raw material purchases will not necessarily follow the pattern of sales as implied by the 'matching' of income and costs. Some materials may be subject to minimum order requirements or, for example, expected price increases or possible shortages might make it desirable to build up buffer stocks. Also the rate at which raw materials are purchased will be affected by any seasonal or strategic run-down or build-up of stocks of finished goods.

In manufacturing businesses of any size, a separate manufacturing budget is needed both to maintain financial control of the manufacturing process and to enable cash flow consequences to be calculated (Figure 2.6).

Rent and business rates

Rent and rates are items of expenditure that are usually paid in advance in one amount or two or more instalments. The sums involved are usually known in advance and budgets will simply allocate such overhead costs as weekly or monthly charges spread evenly throughout the year.

However, cash flow will not be affected evenly. Allowance has to be made for the timing of payments and also for the fact that any increase in rent payable in advance will impact sooner on the cash flow than on the profit statement.

Taxation

All businesses are required to pay tax on their profits – not those profits shown in the accounts but another figure adjusted for various reliefs, allowances, disallowances and apportionments laid down in tax law.

Tax is a complicated subject best dealt with by an expert. But for cash flow statement purposes it is enough to know that a profit-

Madeup Engineering Company
Manufacturing budget – first quarter 1993

Pump casings: Stocks of finished casings	Jan. no.	Feb. no.	Mar. no.	Total no.
Opening stocks of finished goods	5,500	9,300	1,400	5,500
Manufactured during month	16,300	17,100	16,000	49,400
Total available	21,800	26,400	17,400	54,900
Pump casings sold during month	12,500	25,000	13,300	50,800
Closing stocks of finished goods	9,300	1,400	4,100	4,100

Pump casings: Stocks of raw materials	£	£	£	£
Opening stock of raw materials	12,600	8,950	10,700	12,600
Purchased during month	4,500	10,300	2,400	17,200
Total available	17,100	19,250	13,100	29,800
Used for manufacture (50p each)	8,150	8,550	8,000	24,700
Closing stocks of raw materials	8,950	10,700	5,100	5,100

Raw materials – cash flow calculation – first quarter 1993

Pump casings: Payments for raw materials	Total (£)	Jan. (£)	Feb. (£)	Mar. (£)
November 1992 purchases £5,000 plus VAT	5,875	5,875	—	—
December 1992 purchases £10,600 plus VAT	12,455	—	12,455	—
January 1993 purchases £4,500 plus VAT	5,287	—	—	5,287
February 1993 purchases £10,300 plus VAT	12,103	—	—	—
March 1993 purchases £2,400 plus VAT	2,820	—	—	—
Total		5,875	12,455	5,287

Figure 2.6 *Manufacturing budget*

able business will be required to pay tax based on previous period results in a small number of instalments whose dates and amounts can be estimated by whoever is looking after the tax affairs.

Value Added Tax

VAT affects cash flow in two ways. First, as explained above, except for some relatively minor items of disallowable expenditure (a charge for the private benefit element of company car expenditure being the prime example), VAT does not result in a profit or loss to the business. It is therefore excluded from the income and expenditure figures in accounts and from the corresponding budgets.

But since VAT is very much a reality when it comes to raising, receiving and settling invoices, VAT must usually be added to budgeted costs and income to arrive at the cash flow equivalent – the exceptions are businesses too small to be VAT registered traders or invoices for zero-rated goods such as books or children's clothes or exempt services such as financial services.

The second way in which VAT affects cash flow is that settlements of the difference between VAT charged to customers and by suppliers must be made at regular intervals with Customs and Excise.

For most businesses this means paying a substantial amount once every three months. And although this will be no more than has been charged to customers, payment for invoices issued just prior to the end of a VAT accounting period may not have been received by the time VAT is due to Customs.

For the cash flow forecast to be anywhere near the mark it is essential for estimates to be included for the amount and timing of VAT settlements.

Wages and PAYE

Employers are obliged to operate the Paye As You Earn (PAYE) system of tax deduction and to make a National Insurance contribution for each employee. This entails deducting tax and National Insurance from wages, paying over the net amount to employees and keeping back the balance, plus the employer's National Insurance contribution, for payment to the Inland Revenue.

In cash flow terms, therefore, wages are a two-stage affair. Net wages, the major part of the payment, are paid at the end of the appropriate week or month. But the tax and NI element, usually about a third of the total, is due to the Inland Revenue midway through the following month.

Bound to be wrong

The only thing certain about budgets and forecasts is that they are certain to be wrong.

Why then go to all the trouble of preparing them?

The answer is that, if done properly, they will be a reasonably accurate representation of current expectations. Second, and more to the point, budgets are part of a process of negotiation – in both senses of the word. They help the business to negotiate dangers by marking out where hidden rocks may lie. And they assist owners, managers, advisers and financial backers to negotiate between themselves how best to use resources.

Like most things in life, a business plan will be a compromise between different options.

The business might like to expand fast but this means spending money to develop new products. In the mean time it needs to fund increased sales of existing products, offer pay rates that will keep and attract skilled staff, replace worn out machinery and reward its owners. It can borrow from bankers but does not want to be weighed down with high interest charges that will be a drain on future profits.

Not everything can be done at once. There are as many constraints as opportunities.

Planning and control

Budgets and forecasts, of which the cash flow statement is an essential element, can be used to work out the likely outcome of different courses through this maze.

The first draft of a budget is rarely the last. Once committed to paper, weaknesses and possibilities for improvement are almost certain to become obvious in any plan. The final result will be too low, the cash needs for August too high or the demands on machine running times unrealistic.

This is where the negotiation comes in. A new target for sales here, staggering capital spending there, and the plan comes into focus.

It does not stop there. While the cash flow statement will identify periods when something needs to be done to bolster cash resources, it, like other budget statements, is a means of both planning and control.

At the planning stage a check can be made that the level of trading anticipated will lead to a profit – and, if not, this will give managers the opportunity to identify ways of increasing income or of making economies. The budget can be recalculated on various premises to see if the business would be better off, say, by reducing its prices to generate a higher volume of sales. Or what if it increased or reduced the workforce, so placing less or more reliance on overtime?

Budgets also allow managers to ensure that needed resources are in place.

Ironically, budgets themselves become part of the means of obtaining additional resources, when needed. A well-presented budget and cash flow statement will form an essential feature of any representation made to bankers or other financial backers requesting increased borrowing. Besides the potential profit, these statements, and the cash flow statement in particular, will have to demonstrate the business's ability to meet the proposed repayment schedule.

Once finalised, budgets become part of the control mechanism. By comparing actual results achieved with previously set budgets any unexpected aspects of trading will be identified quickly. An analysis of these variances will allow business owners and managers to pinpoint where action is needed to stimulate income, control costs or improve cash flow.

3. Long-term issues

By definition, cash flow problems are short term and short lived – or terminal. But the causes are often deep rooted and long term. Some even go back to the very moment a business was conceived. The way a business is structured, how it is financed and the manner in which it equips itself with the necessary tools of the trade all have a permanent or long-term effect on cash flow.

In Figure 1.4 these were the long-term parts of the financial structure covered by the top half of the outline balance sheet (blocks A and B).

Business format

Businesses come in many different guises but most often they are one-man-band 'sole traders', partnerships or limited companies. There are pros and cons to each format, and also long-term finance and cash flow consequences (Figure 3.1).

A person becomes a sole trader simply by offering his or her trade or professional services for payment. No formal authorisation is needed, there are no legal necessities to go through.

But neither is a distinction drawn between the individual's personal and business finances. A sole trader is responsible for the entire debts of his or her business and, if the worst happens, must sell personal possessions to settle those debts.

A partnership is similar except that each partner is individually responsible. So if one partner runs off, the other is left holding the entire can.

A limited company, on the other hand, is in law a separate being.

	Sole trader	Partnership	Limited company
Formal requirements			
Formal setting-up procedure	No	No, but partnership agreement advisable	Yes
Annual audit required	No	No	Yes
Annual filing of accounts	No	No	Yes
Owner/investor protections and responsibilities			
Limited liability	No	No	Yes
Separation of ownership and management responsibilities	No	No	Yes
Owner/investor restrictions			
Minimum capital required	No	No	Yes – for plcs
Maximum number of equity investors	Yes – by definition	Yes	Yes – except listed companies
Restrictions on profit distributions	No	No	Yes
Taxation			
Tax on all profits	Yes at personal rates	Yes at personal rates	Yes at company rates
Tax on distributions of profits to owners	No	No	Yes, but can be set against future tax
Investors			
Continuity of business when change of owners	No	No	Yes
Different classes of equity investor possible	No	No	Yes

Figure 3.1   *Comparison of different business formats*

It is created by a formal legal process and is owned by shareholders in proportion to the number of shares they hold. This 'equity stake' entitles shareholders to a share of profits. Even so, their liability for the debts of the company is limited to the amount they have paid or agreed to pay for shares. Creditors cannot call on shareholders to dip into personal resources to meet company debts.

Having its own identity, a company has its own tax to pay and its own legal responsibilities and duties – one of which is to file on public record annual accounts prepared in accordance with specific reporting rules and audited by a registered auditor. The attraction of the sole trader or partnership business format is that it is simple to establish and is not subject to the sometimes demanding provisions of the Companies Acts.

Tax advantages

The sole trader or partnership set-up can have tax advantages for the individuals concerned. It allows a little more room for manoeuvre and, for example, owners with losses from other business activities may set these against taxable profits. But equally there can be tax disadvantages which act against accumulating profits within the business.

The owner or owners of businesses operating as a sole trader or partnership will be taxed as individuals on the whole of their share of profits, at higher rates if appropriate, whether or not those profits are actually withdrawn from the business.

Personal assets

Lack of limited liability for sole traders and partners in partnerships can have dire consequences if things go wrong. However, in the mean time the fact that the business is backed by personal assets may make it easier to persuade providers of credit and finance to allow time to pay or access to funds.

And in any case, many owner–directors of companies are asked by their bankers to provide a personal guarantee for business overdrafts, which means that their limited liability protection is in any case eroded to this extent.

New investors

Companies, however, have a significant advantage over unincorporated businesses when it comes to bringing in new investors or selling off part of their activities. Since they are separate entities in their own right, withdrawal or introduction of shareholders does not affect continuity. Shareholders can safely put money into the business without having to take an active part in management – that is the role of directors who are appointed by the shareholders and who have specific legal responsibilities – but in the knowledge that their liability is limited and their entitlement to a share of profits certain. Companies are also flexible structures that can allow for different classes of equity investor including, for example, preferential shareholders who may have first but limited call on profits.

Formalities of preparing annual accounts may appear onerous but, in practice, all businesses must prepare accounts of some kind. And the existence of fully audited annual accounts will be of assistance in satisfying the information needs of backers and would-be backers and in providing the level of assurance required.

Like sole traders and partnerships, companies are obliged to pay tax on the whole of their profits (as computed under the tax rules). But this is always at the special rate for small companies or, at most, the standard company rate – never at the highest level of personal tax.

There is also a payment of Advanced Corporation Tax to be made on distributions of profit, although this can be set against future tax demands.

Adequate funding

So returning to the seafaring analogy, a sole trader is equivalent to the boat-owner plying his or her trade, a company to a group of merchant adventurers who together buy a boat but leave its running to a professional captain. One or more of these adventurers might want to apply for the position of captain or first mate but, even if appointed, will be obliged to look after the interests of all the backers.

Business format therefore affects both the number of investors likely to be involved – there are rules restricting the numbers that may be involved in both partnerships and small companies – their involvement and the terms on which they invest. It also affects the availability and likely sources of finance.

Whatever the business format chosen, the most important rule is that the business should be adequately funded and, in particular, should have long-term funds available to meet long-term commitments.

The higher the proportion of funding that comes from borrowing rather than capital injection or retained profits – the higher the 'gearing' – the more volatile the financial structure. It is often good to have high gearing in times of high inflation but dangerous in times of high interest rates and tight margins. Getting the financial structure and long-term financing wrong will inevitably lead to cash flow problems at some stage.

Financing fixed assets

Fixed assets (those buildings, vehicles, machines, bits of furniture and equipment required to operate any business) are needed on a more or less permanent basis. Thus the means of securing their use must also be for the longer term. It is dangerous from a cash flow point of view to use an overdraft which the bank could in theory ask to be repaid tomorrow to, say, finance purchase of a piece of plant which has a payback period of ten years.

Of course, acquiring use of an asset does not necessarily mean purchasing that asset. Many take the view, when it comes to premises, for example, that they are in business to trade and not to indulge in property speculation. They therefore lease their property rather than buy a freehold.

All businesses require long-term finance to acquire the fixed assets they need to operate and to have sufficient working capital. This finance can come from equity investors, the business itself, bankers, even suppliers. But if the potential for cash flow problems is to be avoided, it is important to match the most appropriate source to the need. In particular, long-term requirements should be met by long-term facilities.

Other considerations are whether or not interest is payable and, if so, whether the rate is fixed in advance, whether assets must be pledged and whether a degree of management control will be surrendered.

From a control point of view it will be helpful if the level and timing of repayments can be scheduled in advance.

Source of finance	Term – long or short?	Repayment – fixed schedule?	Interest – fixed or variable?	Security – assets pledged?	Control – equity interest?
Accumulated profits	Long	No repayment	No interest	No	No
Bank overdraft	Short, repayable on demand	No	Variable	Yes, usually fixed and floating charge	No, but bank will monitor trading
Equity capital	Long	No repayment	No interest but dividends may rise	No	Yes, if additional shareholders or partners brought in
Hire purchase	Long, usually two, three or five years	Yes	Fixed	Yes, but only asset subject of HP	No
Leasing	As HP	Yes	Fixed	Ownership stays with lessor	No
Long-term loans	Long	Yes, but interest likely to vary	Variable	Yes, probably a range of assets	No
Trade creditors	Short	No, depends on supplier's credit control	No interest	No	No, but a poor reputation for paying may limit scope

Figure 3.2 *Financing long-term needs*

As usual there are advantages and disadvantages to this approach. Finance and cash flow may be helped initially since a smaller lump-sum payment – or no initial payment at all – will need to be found. And the amount and timing of future payments will be fixed and not subject to the vagaries of interest rate movements. Over the longer term the business may end up with a weaker balance sheet and be faced with increasing rents; an appreciating freehold property is a valuable asset which can be written up in value and, if necessary, pledged to gain additional finance. If a business does decide, or has no option but to buy fixed assets rather than lease, it is faced with the problem of raising the necessary finance from the most appropriate of a choice of sources (Figure 3.2).

Accumulated profits

A business which is able to finance fixed asset purchases from its own accumulated profits is in the happy position of having the cheapest form of finance possible: there is no outlay on interest and the cost is limited to the income lost by not investing the money elsewhere. Even so, to avoid adverse cash flow consequences the profits must already have been realised and be sitting in a bank account, or be on the point of realisation.

Bank overdraft

Overdrafts are repayable on demand and, as such, are short-term facilities which should be used to finance working capital requirements rather than fixed asset purchases. They do have the advantage of being, usually, one of the cheaper forms of finance especially since interest is charged on the actual amount outstanding from day to day rather than on a total loan figure.

Equity capital

Using additional equity capital – money introduced by the owner or owners – has many advantages. Not least is the effect on the balance sheet which is strengthened, and on the profit and loss account.

Profits will not be affected by interest payments – proprietors,

partners and shareholders take their reward as a share of profit
– but should benefit from new investment.

An improved trading record will in turn help when new loans are
required in the future. Financiers are likely to prove more willing
to come forward and to quote the most competitive interest rates.

Against this the existing owner or owners must set the personal
cost of finding the money required and/or the possible dilution of
their stake in the business by the introduction of others.

Venture capital, money provided by outside professional financiers in return for a stake in profits, is often used as a means of
starting or expanding a business. The venture capitalists accept a
greater risk than providers of secured loans but expect in return
to benefit by more than they would by taking a straight interest
payment – and also to have some say in the running of the business.

Hire purchase

Hire purchase is a useful means of financing fixed asset purchases
since it is freely available and matches or tends to match the term
of the loan to the life of the asset. Control of cash flow is assisted
since the amount and timing of payments is known in advance,
although interest rates charged tend to be higher than, say, for an
overdraft or bank loan.

Leasing

Leasing is very similar to hire purchase when it comes to acquiring plant and equipment, furniture, and vehicles – the main practical difference being in the small print, which means that
technically the asset remains the property of the lessor throughout the period of the lease, and in the VAT consequences (see
above).

When it comes to premises, however, there is the problem of
negotiating and budgeting for rent reviews which will fall due at
regular intervals. Directors or principals in businesses taking on
property leases may well find themselves asked to give personal
guarantees which, under current UK law, can be activated even
after a continuing lease has been assigned to another business.

Long- term loans

Bank and other longer-term loans provide a means of matching the period of the loan to the life of the asset being acquired. From a cash flow point of view they have the advantage of an agreed repayment schedule although the interest element will almost certainly be variable. It is possible also that a bank loan will involve pledging assets other than those being acquired and to this extent will place limits, or at least controls, on future borrowing.

Trade creditors

Relying on the slow payment of bills is usually a cheap but highly dangerous way of financing longer-term requirements. Some businesses, for example supermarkets which have an almost immediate turnover of goods, can achieve more or less permanent negative working-capital requirements but for most any funds made available this way are temporary.

Investment appraisal

Business is a matter of using money to make more money. Although the financial structure of a business and the sources of finance chosen to fund its activities are important to overall performance and cash flow, both at the outset and as the years go by, there is another overriding consideration. Will use of the money invested by owners or borrowed from financiers bring a higher return than its cost?

It is no use setting up a business that can never produce a return on capital of more than 2 per cent before finance charges when interest rates are unlikely to dip below 10 per cent. Likewise it is no use buying a new piece of machinery that will reduce manufacturing costs in each of the next five years by £1,000 when the interest paid out will average £2,000 each year. However well a business is funded at the outset, such decisions will inevitably lead to a long-term drain on cash resources and those funds will run out.

It follows that an essential element of business management, and cash flow management, is effective investment appraisal.

Payback

This means that, prior to any decision to purchase or lease new capital equipment, a review must be undertaken to show whether, on paper at least, the move would be profitable.

There are various techniques for assessing the worth of capital investment, ranging from the simple to the sophisticated. But all involve some estimation of the costs and income and the cash flow that will result.

At the simplest level are return on investment and payback period criteria.

Return on investment involves calculating the average profit (or saving) likely to result from using the new equipment and expressing this as a percentage of the cost. If the percentage is higher than the average interest rates the business is likely to pay and/or reaches predetermined targets, then by this criterion it is worth while.

Payback period is simply a matter of dividing the total cost by the average net cash gain each year. The idea is that this gives an indication of the degree of risk to which the business will be exposed. A long payback period means the risk is higher since the business is exposed to possible interest rate hikes or to increased competition, technical innovation or changes in the market it is serving.

Discounted cash flow

The more sophisticated methods of investment appraisal are based on what is known as the 'discounted cash flow' or 'net present value' method. The principle is the same in both, only the method of presenting the result differs.

As the name implies, this is concerned with the amount and timing of cash flows resulting from an investment. It is based on the notion that money in the hand today is worth more than money in the hand next year. The difference is the amount that could be earned by use of that money in the intervening period. So all cash flows are discounted back to a present value to arrive at a net positive – or negative – total inflow or outflow expected for the investment.

Cash flow statements

The importance of this last method is twofold. First it provides a sophisticated means of assessing the worth of capital investment – and thereby of avoiding a drain on cash resources caused by imprudent purchases of capital equipment.

Second, it emphasises the cash flow significance of capital spending.

Purchases of capital equipment are one of the most likely causes of violent fluctuations in cash flow. But adverse consequences can be avoided in the long term by effective investment appraisal and appropriate choice of financing, and in the shorter term by making the timing convenient to suit expected cash flow.

Whatever the method of appraisal used, no capital commitment should be entered into until its consequences have been written into the cash flow statement and seen to be feasible.

4. Make the most of what you've got

Effective cash flow management means making the most of all the resources under your control. Fixed assets must be fully utilised, working capital kept to the minimum and any surplus cash put to good use.

Any unused office block, idle piece of machinery or excess stock means there is more money tied up in the business than is needed – money that could be used to reduce the overdraft or placed in an interest-earning account.

All these things also impinge upon profits. But they hit cash flow first.

Fixed assets

Controlling and improving cash flow therefore does not mean simply keeping an eye on bankings and making suppliers wait for payment. It requires constant vigilance and calls for systems that monitor potential waste at every level.

When it comes to fixed assets, as discussed in the last chapter, that system should swing into action even before the decision is made to acquire a new building, piece of plant or vehicle. By insisting that new assets are acquired only when they pass the investment appraisal test and can offer at least the agreed minimum return, businesses are eliminating some causes of potential waste.

But it doesn't stop there.

Assets are there to earn a profit. If they do not live up to expectations, do not earn sufficient to cover interest and other overhead costs, then they are a drain on cash flow.

Doing the job

Comparing results with budgets and using ratios to monitor performance helps businesses to make sure that assets are doing the job they were bought to do (Figure 4.1). An even more direct approach is simply to make it somebody's responsibility to walk around the business from time to time to make note of any piece of equipment, any area of office or factory floor, any vehicle that is not in use.

Some items and areas will be out of use some of the time by design, but not all.

An unused machine or vehicle can be sold to realise cash, or at least to put an end to further finance payments. It may be possible to let or even sell off unused office, factory or warehouse space – again to bring in cash.

Property speculator

But more than this, all fixed assets – vehicles, plant, equipment, buildings – are a potential source of cash whether fully utilised or not. They can be pledged to secure loans or sold and leased back.

Buildings are an obvious example. If fully paid for, or worth more than any outstanding loan secured against them, the equity value can be wholly or partly released. Either a new or additional loan can be negotiated or the building could be sold to a finance company and leased back.

If you own your business premises you are a property speculator as well as a trader. Is this the best approach? Many businesses decide they can earn more from trading than from property speculation and would prefer to lease rather than own premises. That way they can use in the business cash that would otherwise be tied up in property.

Ratios and percentages offer an easy means of checking on key areas (see Chapter 9 for a fuller explanation). Below are some ratios that could be used to monitor asset utilisation. They are not the only candidates and others may be more suitable for your particular business.

Whichever indicators you use, there should be an explanation for any marked change from one period to another or between different divisions or companies.

	Ratio	Explanation
Overall		
Return on assets	Profit as a percentage on net assets	A measure of overall efficiency but affected by pricing policy
Asset turnover	Sales per £ of net assets	A measure of efficiency in and using assets and liabilities
Asset mix	Buildings, plant and vehicles, each as a percentage of total net assets	Shows relative level of investment in each category of asset
Asset growth	This period's total net asset figure as a percentage of last's.	Shows whether or not investment is keeping up with level of wear as measured by depreciation
	New investment as a percentage of sales	Shows whether investment is keeping up with sales
Buildings		
Efficiency	Sales per £ of investment in buildings	Usually, the higher the better
Usage	Plant (£) per square foot, and employees per square foot	If the figures dip there may be spare space
Growth	Current investment in buildings as percentage of last period's	Shows whether or not investment is keeping up with level of wear as measured by depreciation
Output	Sales per square foot	Usually, the higher the better
Plant and equipment		
Efficiency	Sales per £ of investment in plant	Usually the higher the better
	Repairs and maintenance per £1,000 of investment	Is plant becoming old and inefficient?
Usage	Hours in use (individual items) as percentage of total working hours	
	Investment per employee	Are employees adequately equipped?
Growth	Current investment in plant as percentage of last period's	Shows whether or not investment is keeping up with level of wear as measured by depreciation
Output	Sales, or value of output per machine hour available	The higher the better

Figure 4.1 *Checking if assets are fully used*

The same principle applies to other types of equipment. Part of the purchase decision will be whether to buy outright, buy on hire purchase or lease the equipment.

But the decision is not irrevocable. There are finance houses that will take over ownership of your existing vehicles and equipment and lease them back to you. That way there is an immediate cash injection.

Obviously, there are costs involved and such a ploy will not be the best thing for every business. But when it comes to managing cash it is important at least to know the option exists.

Debtors too

It is not only major items such as buildings, vehicles or machinery that can be used as security for a loan. Stock and debtors can also be pledged.

Nearly every business with an overdraft gives its bank a 'fixed and floating charge' which covers stock and debtors. There are other ways these current assets can be used to assist cash flow.

Debtors can be 'factored'.

In effect, the sales ledger, or at least the juiciest part of it, is passed over to a factoring house – usually a subsidiary of a bank. This organisation will undertake to collect the money but will advance immediate payment of a large part of each invoice run as issued in return for an interest charge (see page 61).

There are variations on the theme with, in some cases, it not being obvious to customers that the debt has been factored. But the essence of the deal is the same: money is advanced against outstanding debts.

The arrangement is not suitable for every business. Factors do not offer their services to all types or size of firm. And as the bank's floating charge will be out-ranked by the factor's claims, its permission will more than likely be required before a factoring arrangement can be put in place. There are also the costs to be considered.

It is also possible to borrow against larger individual invoices by way of 'invoice discounting'. The difference here is that the discounter is not interested in getting involved in regular management of your sales ledger, only in lending against particular items.

And stock

Stock too is a source of improved cash flow.

Quite apart from the possibility of releasing money tied up in unnecessary stock – stock and debtor control, issues at the heart of short-term cash management, are dealt with in following chapters – stock is a possible source of finance.

Like debtors, stock you hold will almost certainly be pledged against any overdraft. But this is so whether or not you have actually paid your supplier.

Increasing the time you are allowed to pay – effectively borrowing from suppliers – is a simple way of improving the cash position.

It rarely pays simply to hold up payments. That is the way to get your account looked at more critically and to end up being chased harder for settlement. But if you have a good reputation for paying up when invoices are due, you might easily be able to negotiate a longer credit period with one or more suppliers. If you are negotiating on price, why not ask for 60 or 90 days' credit? You may even be able to sell the item and have the money in the bank before you have to settle up.

In the bank

Money comes to money, so they say. But not unless you work at it.

It is very nice to have a credit balance at the bank, but holding more than your immediate needs on credit account is simply a waste.

Cash flow management is not about accumulating the biggest possible bank balance. Far from it. It is about using every possible resource to the utmost – including cash itself.

Again, planning and monitoring are important. Budgets and plans should give an idea of whether credit balances are likely to continue indefinitely, for the medium term, or for only a matter of days. Constantly checking the actual cash position will highlight any unexpected, but almost certainly short-term, jump in balance.

Whatever the situation, the message is 'get it invested'. Options range from putting long-term surpluses into long-term investments such as new – profitable – capital items, even acquisitions of other businesses, to moving it to an interest-bearing account. Short-term surpluses can be made to earn interest even over a day or two or overnight.

It is just as wasteful to have money excess to requirements sitting in a current account as it is to leave a piece of machinery unused. Effective cash flow management means making the most of all the assets at your disposal.

5. Preventing leaks

Like any flow, cash flow can leak away unless channelled, piped or dammed. A precious commodity, cash can seep from all but the tightest of 'tight ships'.

This brings cash flow management into the realms of internal control – the systems of checking and counter-checking, signing and counter-signing that should be in place in any business to prevent errors, theft and waste. The essence of internal control is a division of labour – not always possible in every situation or at all in smaller businesses, but something to aim for.

The idea is that the employee requesting a payment be made should not be the same person who signs the cheque; the person issuing stock should not do so on his or her own authority. To have at least two people involved removes some of the possibility of error and temptation for fraud.

There should be a definite policy for dealing with each of the following problem areas.

Cheque payments

Unwarranted or wrongly timed payments will throw the most carefully planned cash flow out of kilter. Control systems must guard against both possibilities.

Supplier invoices should be considered for payment only if counter-signed or cross-referenced to an official order authorised by the appropriate manager.

If credit is involved, the bookkeeper entering the invoice into the system should check that authorisation and correct credit terms have been recorded.

Computer-based purchase ledgers will provide a list of due payments so that cheques can be drawn. Most importantly, the person keeping the purchase ledger and running off payment schedules should not be the same person who signs the cheques. Likewise, the person drawing up pay slips should not also sign wage cheques.

If the business is any size, it is best to require any company cheque be signed by two authorised people, again as a counter-check. And in signing, each should have in mind the possibilities for fraud and error, including, for example, payments to phantom employees or suppliers.

Credit control

Credit control is so crucial to cash flow management that it warrants separate treatment in the next chapter. But within this area lurk one or two important internal control issues.

First there are the mechanics of actually issuing invoices and statements in good time. There needs to be a system to ensure these are issued for every sale, that no customer is forgotten or overlooked, and that it is issued on time and containing the correct information.

Next there is the question of discounts and credit notes. These represent cash forgone and a proper system of authorisation should be in place.

In particular neither sales people nor those who keep sales ledger records or are responsible for sales ledger receipts should be given a free hand.

Finally, there should be some separation between the receipt of and banking of cheques and the recording of sales ledger transactions.

Expenses claims

Although individually small, expenses can add up to significant amounts whose timing may be uncertain.

Where this is likely to be the case employees should be set budgets and individual spending levels – so that prior authorisation is required for expenditure outside the budget or over an agreed amount.

Repayment of expenses incurred for business purposes should only be made on production to the petty-cash controller of a claim counter-signed by an authorised manager.

One way some firms control expenses is to issue employees with credit cards or other means of payment valid for designated purposes only – such as buying petrol. Provided open-ended credit is not involved, this system has the advantage of incorporating a recording system so that expenditure is detailed on regular statements from the card company. In some instances statements also detail vehicle mileage so that average consumption of petrol can be compared between vehicles and employees.

Invoicing

As mentioned above, invoicing, the issuing of your demands for cash from customers, should command special attention. At the end of the month a day lost in invoicing can mean a month's delay in payment.

An incorrect invoice can also cause delay. As can invoicing the wrong customer.

Part of the internal control system relies on customers to point out when they have been overcharged – undercharging is another matter, and not so likely to come to light as the result of a customer complaint. So it is important both that invoices are sent out speedily and that they are followed up at regular intervals by statements showing any outstanding balance. That way customers cannot say they did not know what was owing and have the opportunity to point out errors quickly.

Petty cash

Petty cash should be kept petty. There is no point having a lot of money sitting around in a tin, or even a safe for that matter. It could be a temptation to thieves, but is certainly 'dead money' that is not earning a return.

Neither, because the sums involved seem small, should a proper control system be ignored.

Petty cash should be one person's responsibility. The amount of cash he or she holds at any one time, added to the value of receipts for claims paid since petty cash was last replenished, should always total the same agreed amount. Thus replenishments will be exactly what has been paid out to bring the total back to the original.

This means it is easy for a responsible manager other than the petty-cash controller to check on the balance from time to time. There should be a policy requiring authorisation by somebody other than the petty-cash controller for all payments, with, if necessary, different levels of authorisation for different amounts.

Purchasing

Placing an order for supplies, services or equipment commits the business to a cash payment further down the line.

The first priority is to make ordering the specific responsibility of one or more people, each with their own level of authority. Nobody other than those given purchasing responsibility should be allowed to commit the business to any purchases.

Each buyer should have a budget within which to operate covering the level of purchases and the price. And each should know the acceptable credit terms and the degree to which they may negotiate on those terms – for example, by accepting a discount for a promise to pay more quickly than usual.

Needless to say, there should be controls to ensure purchase orders are placed only when stocks are low. Holding excessive stock is just as harmful to cash flow as holding excessive petty cash.

Ideally, buyers should operate an ordering system so that any invoice received bears an order reference number. And no invoice should be entered into the purchase ledger unless counter-signed by the buyer.

Sales people

Sales people, whether or not paid on commission, live to make a sale. But enthusiasm to close a deal should not be allowed to overrun cash consequences.

There should be some system in place to make sure sales people know who the bad-risk customers are, and which customers are likely to pay late. If there is little or no prospect of the cash coming in, there is no point making the sale.

If payment is likely to come late, there will be less money in the bank, more interest to pay or less to earn. So there is less scope for discounting prices.

Agreed parameters are needed if credit periods are likely to come into sales negotiations. A huge sale, however profitable, could prove disastrous if a vastly extended credit period is agreed to clinch the deal.

Likewise, there should also be agreed limits on discounts that can be offered and strict control on credit notes. It should certainly not be within the sole power of a sales person to issue a credit note. A formal authorisation procedure is needed.

If there is a likelihood of sales people and their clients developing such a close relationship that the interests of the business are in danger of being compromised, it might be wise policy to ensure sales areas or responsibilities are switched from time to time.

Stock control

A fine balance is needed between holding too little stock to meet orders and holding so much that it amounts to a waste of resources. Controlling this is one thing, controlling the people who control the balance is another – and a matter of internal control.

Again the issue comes down to planning, monitoring and levels of authorisation.

Stock should not be available for use willy-nilly. Each type of stock should be the responsibility of a designated person. He or she will issue stock on receipt of suitably authorised requisitions and will have responsibility for maintaining stock levels within agreed limits. If stocks are to be kept to a minimum, the upper limit will reflect maximum expected usage within the likely delivery time plus an agreed safety margin.

Takings

Tight control of all money coming into the business is required.

Most problems arise if this is in cash – notes and coinage, rather than in cheques. It is essential to have an effective cash register system with receipts issued and copies kept on every occasion.

Cheques too can go astray or be incorrectly recorded. If possible have somebody other than the person maintaining the sales ledger log receipt of cheques and, more importantly, in charge of the cash book and bankings.

Ultimately, mistakes will be put right because customers who have paid but who are still chased because their cheques have been mislaid or wrongly recorded will certainly complain.

Whether takings are received as cash or cheques, they should be banked as soon as possible. There should be a system in place to make sure this happens and money does not lie around for a day or two before being banked and while overdraft interest mounts up.

Some types of business that charge customers regular amounts are able to ask for direct-debit authorisations. Where this is possible it should be pursued. Costs of chasing for renewals and payments are cut while collection of cash is speeded up.

Wages

Wages are the biggest regular class of payments many businesses make.

If paid in cash there is a security problem which must be faced. Certainly, cash should be held for the minimum period possible, not more than a few hours. And there must be adequate means of guarding and securing the cash while in transit and on business premises.

Clearly cheques or credit transfers are a more secure means of payment – and all firms have the right to opt for payment by cheque if they wish. But whichever means of payment is chosen, there should be internal checks to ensure the amounts paid over are correct.

If paid hourly or on piecework, the amount claimed should be cross-checked and authorised by a person with management responsibility. Another person should use this information to calculate wages, and a third to make up wage packets or draw cheques.

6. Credit only where it's due

One of the easiest ways to run out of cash is to sell on credit and then let your customers keep the money due to you longer than they should.

Bad debts are obvious losses; long overdue amounts clear problems. They are only part of the picture.

One or two bad debts will probably not hurt as much as allowing all customers a week longer to pay than they are entitled to.

Credit control, then (the means of collecting payment from all customers) is of crucial importance to cash flow.

And no system of credit control can function properly without a number of elements fitted into an overall policy. These elements will cover customer vetting and credit limits, invoicing, credit chasing and debt recovery.

Success will also depend upon having adequate accounting and information systems in place and being able to rely on sales and debtor records.

Accounting records

Unless you know what is owing to you, you have no hope of collecting it.

Credit control starts, therefore, with the accounting system. This must be accurate enough for you to be able to rely on it when chasing payment, and detailed enough to reveal the origin of debts. In the event of an argument about whether or not the debt was actually incurred, you must be able to trace and retrieve documentation.

The system must also be fast enough to eliminate wasted time between sale and invoicing, and flexible enough to throw up anomalies and late payments.

For all but the very smallest concerns the best solution is likely to be installation of a computerised sales ledger. The range of cheap and highly efficient machines and accounting packages now available means there will be at least one to suit almost any firm.

All accounting packages will produce statements at the tap of a few keys. Most, if not all, will churn out a debtors list, differentiating between amounts not yet due, those due and those that are overdue. Such an 'aged debtors list' (Figure 6.1) will provide the

Customer	Total outstanding	Under 30 days	Between 30 days and 60 days	Over 60 days
	£	£	£	£
Ace Pumps	4,750		2,300	2,450
Defoe Water and Gas	8,240	3,280	3,160	1,800
Lixstowe Heaters	3,250			3,250
Promo Cars	31,960	17,860	14,100	
Syke and Wexford Engineering	10,800	6,100	4,700	
Variety Motors	8,200	2,100	3,240	2,860
Total	67,200	29,340	27,500	10,360

Madeup Engineering had total sales of £117,140 in the three months to 31 March or £1,301 per day (£117,140 divided by 90).
Outstanding debtors at £67,200 therefore represent an average 52 days' credit (£67,200 divided by £1,301).

Although this is within the range expected by Madeup, four customers have amounts outstanding over 60 days and should be chased. Lixstowe Heaters, which only has amounts over 60 days outstanding, is a particular cause for concern.

Figure 6.1   *Madeup Engineering Company: aged debtors list – 31 March 1993*

framework for credit chasing. Some systems will even generate chasing letters at the appropriate time.

Computerising the sales ledger also opens the door to a great deal of other analysis which will, for example, help to keep tabs on sales of individual products or in particular areas or by individual sales people.

This information can be used to make sure the business is not becoming too reliant on particular customers or is increasing sales to, say, a particular industry sector with a slow-paying history.

Factoring

Factoring is an option which cuts out some of the accounting and credit-chasing problem altogether.

In essence the deal entails handing over the sales ledger to a factoring company which will undertake to collect payments and will lend against a good proportion of the outstanding amount in the mean time, while providing insurance cover against non-payment.

The catch is that there is, of course, a charge for this service, interest to pay on advances and the need to maintain duplicate sales ledger records. And not every business is keen on its customers knowing it has factored its debts – although a confidential version of the arrangement is available.

Against this, many customers might feel obliged to pay a little quicker if chased by a factoring company with banking connections.

Customer vetting

Whether or not the sales ledger is factored, it is important to know to whom you are selling.

It is not always practical to make enquiries about customers before agreeing to a sale – to delay may mean a loss of business. But where it is feasible to do so, it is wise to insist on formal procedures before opening credit accounts. This shows the customer that you take credit control seriously and should help you to weed out particularly risky prospects.

It is a good idea to ask the new customer to suggest a reasonable credit limit, to say whether his or her business is incorporated as a company or operates as a sole trader or partnership, to name its bank and to provide trade references. Ideally, you should ask for, say, the names of two other suppliers with whom the new customer deals.

It is unlikely the customer will give names of suppliers he or she does not pay promptly. Nevertheless, a letter should be sent asking for confirmation that your customer is indeed also their customer, and asking whether the referee knows of any reason why you should not grant credit to the limit mentioned in the letter.

Company accounts

If the amount of credit involved is substantial it could be wise to ask also for a banker's reference and to see the latest accounts. Do not forget, though, that accounts concern the past, sometimes reasonably ancient past, rather than the present or the future.

If accounts are not forthcoming, copies of company accounts can be inspected at Companies House in London or Cardiff or obtained, for a fee, from one of the specialist search agencies. Information on file at Companies House will include the names of directors and details of any other directorships they hold. The names of shareholders will be shown as will any charges against assets giving other creditors first call on their sale proceeds should that creditor not be paid.

Accounting information will enable you to see if the business is adequately funded, how highly it is geared and whether there is a safe margin of current assets over current liabilities. (Remember Figure 1.4?)

It is also worth looking at the auditor's report – all companies must file such a report – to see whether a 'qualified' opinion has been given.

Annual accounts provide a means of checking on creditworthiness. The following checklist sets out the most important points to look at.

Question	Where to look	Comment
Is the business incorporated as a company or operated as a sole trader or partnership?	Limited companies must use the word 'limited' in their name. Letterheads must bear a registered number	Liability of the owners to settle company debts is limited to the value of their shares
Who owns the business?	For companies – the annual return filed at Companies House. Unincorporated businesses must display the names of proprietors on letterheads and also at their principal place of business	Companies are owned by their shareholders. Look for major shareholders who work for the business but are not directors – they could be disqualified
Who runs the business?	Details of directors are filed at Companies House. Unincorporated businesses are run by their owners	Look to see other directorships held by directors and whether these companies are still in business
Who can claim what?	The company's register of charges filed at Companies House	The register of charges will show which assets are pledged
Have the accounts been audited?	Check to see if there is an audit report	An audit is compulsory for companies but optional for others
What is the auditor's verdict?	The audit report will accompany the accounts. If the opinion is 'qualified' it will include mention of the reason	Look for words like 'subject to', which signify uncertainty, 'except for', which signify disagreement
Is the business profitable?	Look at the profit and loss account	Small companies are excused filing a profit and loss account. Look at trading profit and pre-tax profit
Is the financial structure sound?	Balance sheet	Look at the amount of equity capital. Check gearing
Are short-term finances healthy?	Balance sheet	See if current assets exceed current liabilities. Check size of overdraft
Are there any worries about the future?	Look for notes about uncertainties and contingent liabilities	Account should provide for all known liabilities

Figure 6.2 *Accounts checklist*

If the auditor draws attention to use of the 'going concern' basis of accounting and says his or her opinion is 'subject to' this basis being appropriate, the auditor is in fact expressing uncertainty about the future viability of the business.

Beyond this, it is possible to gain credit-rating advice from commercial specialists in the field, such as Dun and Bradstreet. Also, many trade associations maintain information about creditworthiness. If you are in a business sector covered by such an association or federation, you have a valuable source of information – and also a strong tool in the collection process. It is worth letting customers know of any such connections since it will be very persuasive in convincing them of the need to maintain a good payment record.

Having gone through this procedure, a credit limit should be fixed for the customer and stuck to until a review is requested. Irrespective of the timing of orders and payments, the customer should know that this is the maximum amount you will allow to be outstanding at any one time.

Protective measures

Besides being careful to vet customers prior to agreeing to allow credit, there are other protective measures which can be incorporated into policy.

Where contracts are large, involve purchase of special materials or specially made items, it is not unreasonable to ask for a deposit in advance and perhaps also for progress payments. In this way the credit risk will be reduced and cash flow helped.

If goods rather than services are involved, it may be wise to incorporate a 'reservation of title' clause into your standard terms of trade and to print this on the back of invoices. Such a clause states that title to the goods concerned does not change hands until the invoice has been paid. The idea is that, should the customer go broke, the goods cannot be sold off by a liquidator to the benefit of other creditors such as the bank, but come back to you.

Clearly this is a legal device and the advice of a solicitor in drafting a suitable clause is advisable.

Another option is to take out credit insurance. This will not take away the problem of slow payers but will at least provide cover in the event of a customer going broke. Insurance costs money, of course, and only approved customers will be covered. So cost and inconvenience needs to be weighed against risk.

Sales versus caution

In fact, fine judgement has to be exercised all along the line when deciding what information is required, what checks will be made and what protection demanded before a credit sale can be agreed.

It is no good having watertight credit control if, as a result, nobody buys from you because they are put off by all the palaver. On the other hand, record sales are worthless unless and until the money turns up.

What is required is a sensible balance between caution and risk-taking so that, it is hoped, all the most obvious and dangerous risks are eliminated while no, or hardly any, customers are put off by your procedures.

If you have a credit policy, stick to it. Check that credit limits have not been breached before making deliveries. If they have, explain the situation to the customer as quickly and as clearly as possible.

If they know the rules, most customers will not object to an inadvertent breach being pointed out and will bring their account back into line.

The same attitude must be applied to the collection process. It must be firm but not offensive – otherwise there will be little hope of repeat business – persistent but not unreasonable.

The paperwork

Slow or sloppy paperwork creates late payment.

Every day lost between delivery of goods and despatch of an

invoice is likely to be at least a day's delay in payment. If a sale is completed on the last day of the month and the invoice not issued until the first of the following, there could easily be a month's delay.

Likewise, invoices that are queried will be paid later than those that are not. So it is important that quantities and prices should be correct, discounts as agreed and order numbers obvious.

Wherever possible it is good policy to work on the basis of signed orders. If this is impractical, sales people should at least be required to complete the equivalent of an order, filling in the customer's authorisation details, any special requirements and the price and discounts agreed.

This information, together with despatch details, should form the basis of an invoice generated just as quickly as possible after delivery. Invoices should bear sufficient information to enable the customer to check all relevant details, and should recite credit terms and any special conditions such as reservation of title until payment has been made.

Invoices should be followed up with statements on a set day each month.

Statements

Statements perform two tasks. First they confirm the state of the account and bring, or should bring, any missing or incorrect invoices or overlooked payments to the attention of the customer.

Second, they act as a reminder that a payment is due – and to this end many businesses attach a confirmation-of-payment slip so that this can be torn off and sent with the cheque, thereby identifying the payer and the particular invoices being settled.

It is helpful if the statement highlights invoices due and overdue for payment and reminds the customer of the terms on which they have agreed to do business.

In many computerised sales ledger systems the statement run is a means of matching off previous payments against corresponding invoices so that the account is cleaned up and left with outstanding invoices only. It is therefore an important part of the system quite apart from being a means of communication.

It should act as a trigger for running off an aged debtors list, which in turn will activate the chasing process.

Methods of payment

The point of credit control is to collect cash in as speedily as possible.

It follows that the payment process should be made as simple as possible for customers. Cheques, postal orders, credit and debit card payments, direct debits, cash, standing orders, credit transfers, money orders, should all be welcome. The object is to get the money into the bank as quickly as possible.

A proviso is that a business decision has to be made about the relative cost of, say, accepting card payments, against the possible loss of business or cost of delay in not doing so. But do not forget that quite apart from the saving in interest, having money in advance, or at least guaranteed on time, cuts out or down on the risk of not being paid at all.

When credit accounts are opened it is sensible to ask the knew customer how accounts are to be settled. In this way any necessary details can be exchanged well in advance of settlement day and administrative delay avoided.

Cash discounts

Prompt payment is one of the reasons that some firms, in the past many more firms, offer a cash discount for payment within a specified time. While cash discounts may work for some it is potentially dangerous. First there is the risk of giving customers the idea that they can pay on time and get the discount or alternatively pay late. And once the discount has been forgone, how late does not matter.

Second, it is not unknown for businesses to claim cash discount whether or not they are entitled to it. They work on the assumption that the amount involved is likely to be so small that it will not be worth chasing or taking action over.

Third, it can work out to be an expensive exercise – and much more so if a constant watch is not kept on the comparison between the discount offered and current interest rates.

If offering cash discount of 'only' 1.5 per cent speeds up the average collection period by two weeks, you are in fact paying the equivalent of up to 39 per cent per annum interest (52 divided by 2, multiplied by 1.5 per cent).

Chasing

There will always be some customers who need chasing for payment.

Invoices can be overlooked or lost, sent to the wrong address or accidentally thrown away, invoicing mistakes can happen, customers can face their own cash flow difficulties, and some will simply try to get away with what they can. So some form of follow-up on overdue accounts, in addition to the regular mailing of statements, is an essential part of credit control.

There are various options available. It is best to select a preferred combination, with timing intervals, and stick to it. In broad terms the options are to chase by telephone, by letter, by use of an outside agency or a combination of any two or of all three. At the end of the line will come legal action.

Chasing by telephone (Figure 6.3) takes time and patience but can be effective, particularly where customers are well known. The rule might be to allow three phone calls before considering legal action. The first would be a friendly reminder, the second a firmer demand and the last a warning of action.

The person making the call should identify who they are talking to, make sure they have an appropriate level of authority, establish there is no legitimate reason why payment has been withheld and elicit an undertaking the outstanding invoice or invoices will

Excuses for holding up payment of invoices are legendary. Below are some of the more common types of excuse together with a suggested response. In all cases it is important to keep a record of the conversation, to note the name of the person you are talking to and to obtain, if possible, an undertaking of some action by a specific date.

Excuse	Response
I have not seen/received your invoice	I will send you a copy today and will telephone you tomorrow to make sure it has arrived. The invoice was shown on statements sent you and is now overdue for payment. May I check your address?
There is a query on this invoice	With whom have you raised the query? I presume this was in writing, in which case please give me the date and your reference. And what was the amount involved? I will find out how this is being dealt with. Meanwhile please send part payment for the undisputed amount
The goods were damaged on arrival	With whom have you raised this matter? Unfortunately the terms of our insurance, which are stated quite clearly on our delivery notes, require notification within seven days of delivery. As you have not complied with this condition I am sorry to say we cannot now put the matter right and must ask you for payment which is now overdue
You missed off my special discount/the price was not as quoted	We have your signed order which I will of course check. I will make sure a copy is sent to you tonight together with any credit note due. In the mean time please send payment for the part of the invoice which is not in dispute and which is now overdue
I have been promised a credit note	Who made this promise and for what reason? I will of course check this and send you any credit note that is due. In the mean time I must ask you to pay the part of the invoice which is not in dispute
We always pay late, you never complained before	As a regular customer you will know our terms of trade are stated quite clearly on our order forms and invoices. If we have not chased you before it must have been an oversight because we operate a policy of strict credit control. I must ask you to send payment immediately
I will deal with this shortly	The amount is now overdue so I would ask you to make this a matter of urgency. Can you deal with this today? If not today, when?
You will be included in our next run	When is your next payment run? Presumably you would not object if somebody comes to collect the cheque that day?
The only person who can sign cheques is away	Who is that person? When will they return? I will telephone them that day to remind them that payment is overdue
Our accountant only comes in odd days	Who is the accountant? What days is he/she in? Where else can I reach the accountant? I will telephone the day you say as a final reminder
A cheque has already been sent	Please tell me how much for, the date and the cheque number. If it has not arrived by tomorrow I will telephone to let you know
I am unable to pay at present	What is the reason? I can understand that you may have short-term problems and will therefore accept part payment now. How much can you pay me today, and when can I expect the balance? *Or* – I will accept post-dated cheques totalling the amount due
If you want my business you had better stop chasing me	Naturally we wish to maintain good relations with customers. This is why we state our terms of trade clearly on all relevant paperwork. We cannot continue to supply customers who do not keep within these terms. I must insist on payment of the overdue amount
The business has ceased trading	What date did you cease trading? What arrangements are being made to settle outstanding debts? What is the name and address of the receiver/liquidator/bankruptcy trustee?

Figure 6.3   *What to say*

be settled by an agreed date. If this cannot be achieved, some other action should be agreed, again within a specified time.

The customer should be reminded of the credit terms to which he or she has agreed. It may be helpful to remind the customer of their credit limit and that further supplies cannot be made while overdue invoices remain outstanding. And queries should be dealt with and cleared up as quickly as possible.

In the event of a dispute, payment should be sought for any amounts that are not being questioned.

If the customer says he or she is unable to pay, it may be reasonable to take a sympathetic line. It helps neither you nor your customer if they are forced out of business.

But do not give too much away. Ask for at least a part payment and an agreed schedule for settling the remainder of the debt. Or perhaps accept post-dated cheques which can be banked as they fall due.

Using the telephone has the advantage that queries and problems can be identified and possibly sorted out on the spot.

They also have a certain nuisance value. Whereas a letter can be binned, a persistent telephone caller has to be dealt with at some time or other. So if there is a choice to be made about who gets paid first, it might be that troublesome person who keeps ringing up.

Letters are more formal

Letters take less time – standard letters can be set up so that only name, address and account details need be changed. They are also more formal and, should the matter go to court, copies provide proof that you have reminded the customer of his or her obligations to pay and given ample opportunities for queries to be raised.

Often a series of two or three letters (Figure 6.4) are sent as a matter of course. The first would simply bring the customer's attention to the fact that an overdue invoice remains unpaid and

Credit control procedures often incorporate two or three standard chasing letters which become progressively more demanding the longer an invoice remains unpaid. Below are examples.

Letter 1
Have you overlooked our invoice?

We notice that invoice number XC101 for £103.50 dated 1 April 1993 remains unpaid. The 30-day credit period we agreed to allow you has now expired, so settlement is overdue.

Please tell us if you have any queries regarding our invoice. Otherwise we look forward to receiving your cheque within seven days.

Letter 2
We are writing to remind you that, despite an earlier reminder, our invoice number XC101 for £103.50 dated 1 April 1993 still remains unpaid.

You are a valued customer whose business we would not wish to lose. However, as we all know, the cost of finance is high. This is why it is company policy to maintain strict credit limits which are constantly reviewed in line with payment experience.

To avoid the possibility of further action on our part, please send payment for the above invoice by return.

Letter 3
Despite previous unanswered reminders, our invoice number XC101 for £103.50 dated 1 April 1993 remains unpaid.

As a member of a trade association whose members have agreed to do everything possible to monitor late payment and enforce recovery of debts we will be obliged to commence legal proceedings should payments not be received by 15 June 1993.

Figure 6.4 *Chasing letters*

asks for payment or notification of any queries. The second would be stronger, draw attention to the consequences of continued delay, and the third would demand payment within a specified time and give notification of legal action should payment not be forthcoming.

Use of letters can be effective, but not nearly so effective if customers get to know the sequence. If you always allow ten days before sending the first letter, another ten before the second, and ten more before the third, the slicker customers will always pay up thirty days late.

So it pays to vary the letters from time to time and to watch out for regular customers who only pay on the limit. They need to be dealt with separately and individually.

Outside agencies

All or some of the above actions can be placed in the hands of an outside agency dealing in credit chasing, either using the telephone, letters or both.

The cost of this might be a 'per-letter' or 'per-client' basis or charged as a percentage of the amount recovered.

Using an agency with an important-sounding name can frighten customers into paying earlier than otherwise. And the discipline of dealing with an outside agency can help you to maintain a proper chasing regime.

The disadvantages include the cost, the possibility that customers might be upset and of misuse on your part.

The longer a debt is allowed to roll, the harder it will be to collect. So do not expect a collection agency to be able to perform miracles by taking on only the oldest and most difficult accounts. It will probably charge more and collect less. The proper use of an agency is as part of a formal collection process that does not extend over too great a period (Figure 6.5).

There will always be some customers who need chasing before they will part with cash and settle their bills. To be effective any credit control policy must include chasing procedures together with a timetable for action. Below is an example timetable.

Document	Action	Comment
Invoice	As soon as delivery note received in accounts	Should include reminder of credit terms
Statements	25th of each month or last working day prior to 25th	Many businesses make payments on the last day of the month. Get in first
Aged debtors list	Run off each Monday	Aged debtors list is trigger for chasing
Letter 1	Send seven days after invoice due for payment	Polite reminder
Telephone call	Seven days after letter 1	Any reason for non-payment? What action does customer intend? Follow up as necessary
Letter 2	Seven days after telephone call	Firm reminder. Inform sales staff of problem with account
Letter 3 (final)	Seven days after telephone call	Last chance. Suspend credit
Pass to solicitor	Seven days after letter 3	Solicitor's letter is last chance of avoiding legal action

Total time
Invoicing to first statement – up to 30 days
Invoicing to first letter – 37 days
Invoicing to first call – 44 days
Invoicing to second letter – 51 days
Invoicing to third letter – 58 days
To placing in legal hands – 65 days

Figure 6.5 *Chasing collection*

Legal proceedings

At some point, with some debts, you will be forced to consider taking legal action.

Be sure at the outset that nobody is likely to win by this. If the debt is proved and the customer forced to pay up, then he or she will have additional costs and interest to pay. But you are unlikely to recover all your expense and certainly not all of the time and energy that has been spent trying to get what is rightfully yours.

There will be delays. And, of course, you will certainly lose a customer – albeit one you would have second thoughts doing business with for the time being anyway.

So legal action is very much a last resort, and one that should be undertaken only after the consequences have been outlined to the customer – probably in a solicitor's letter.

But it is a threat that is only a deterrent if seen to be used on occasions. So to avoid getting a name for being soft on debtors and as a warning to others who might try to avoid payment, it is worth pursuing at least the worst payers through the courts.

Smaller debts can be chased through the small-claims court at modest cost, completing the paperwork yourself if preferred. But if you can make more money running your business than filling in forms, it is likely that a solicitor will be needed.

You will get something back and be seen to be tough. But the best solution is to maintain a system of credit control and chasing that lets very few cases get this far.

Bad debts

Inevitably you will have to write off some debts as irrecoverable.

Some customers will get away with small amounts by refusing to pay or by making a great fuss and complaining about invoices that they know are not worth chasing. Larger businesses sometimes pursue all amounts as a matter of policy. But most take a view on the likelihood of financial advantage when deciding which invoices to chase to the bitter end.

At the very least your policy should be of the 'once bitten twice shy' variety. There is little point doing business with people who are likely to take any profit out of the deal by being difficult about paying. And there is certainly no point in giving discounts to get their business.

Some customers will simply go out of business or go bankrupt. If you see this coming there are a few things you can do – restrict business to cash on delivery only, and perhaps ask for personal guarantees. But after the event there is little that can be done. Of course, a customer just saying that he or she has gone broke is not good enough. Until formal insolvency proceedings have commenced you still have a chance – the best chance probably being to agree some schedule of payments the customer can meet. Your threat is to force official insolvency, something most businesses, especially unincorporated businesses and individuals, would much prefer to avoid.

Again, it is a situation in which there are few winners. When a business fails its assets are sold off to the highest bidder. And since it will be a forced sale, the highest bid is not likely to be that high. Also, the costs of the insolvency have to be met, while outstanding accounts will be more difficult to collect.

If your errant customer is a company, formal insolvency will involve receivership – in which, in theory at least, the company still has some chance of survival – or liquidation. In either case the most likely outcome is that the assets of the business are sold off to pay creditors in a set order. First come 'secured creditors' – those that have charges against assets; then 'preferred creditors' – such as the Inland Revenue; lastly, 'unsecured creditors'.

Since normal trade debts come in the last category and are at the bottom of the line for payment, you can hope for little or nothing by way of settlement.

If the customer is a sole trader or partnership, you have slightly more chance of payment since you have a call on personal as well as business assets. But personal bankruptcy will involve only part payment of debts – so much in the pound – even at best. In either event it is important to ensure that the receiver, liquidator or trustee has details of your outstanding account. This is not so much in hope of being paid – although you never know, some cash might eventually come your way – as being certain to be able to enforce what rights you have and to claim back the VAT element of the debt.

If you include a reservation of title clause in your terms of trade, the receiver or liquidator must be made aware of this as soon as possible. There may well be an argument over your rights to the goods involved. But unless you make a claim – and a stand – you will certainly lose out.

Businesses must pay Customs and Excise the net VAT collected, that is the VAT on sales less the VAT paid out on purchases and business expenses. In most businesses of any size, the VAT element of sales is counted when an invoice is issued, not when the cash is received.

This means that if you have a bad debt you will probably already have paid over to Customs the VAT element of the invoice or invoices. But with a certificate from a receiver, liquidator or trustee you can claim back this VAT by setting the amount against what is due at the time of your next return.

Without this certificate it is necessary to wait a year before re-claiming the VAT – and inclusion on VAT returns can be forgotten.

Smaller businesses can opt to account for VAT on a cash basis – paying over to Customs only the VAT actually received. This is an option worth considering.

If the amount due to you from an insolvent customer is particularly large you may wish to have a say in the way the insolvency is handled. All creditors have a right to attend a creditors meeting where formal decisions, such as the appointment of liquidators and of creditors' committees, are taken.

Unless you feel particularly strongly about the circumstances surrounding the insolvency or have a great deal at stake, it is rarely worth while becoming involved.

It is far better to concentrate on making as certain as possible that you do not do business in future with bad risks and that you collect in what is due to you as speedily as possible.

7. Stock options

Stock is cash. The more you have, the more money is tied up in the business. The faster you process it and sell it on, the quicker you will get your money in.

Most businesses need to carry some stock, some a great deal, to compete in their particular sector.

Certainly, stocks should be kept to a minimum, but that minimum must reflect not only order levels and delivery times. Purchasing and marketing strategy, even production and design policies, all play a significant role.

Stocks come in various forms. Manufacturers and processors are likely to hold stocks the longest. They buy raw materials and parts which, while in the manufacturing process, become work in progress. Finally, they are held as stocks of finished goods. Wholesalers and retailers then take up the chain, buying from manufacturers and holding their goods for resale.

The length of time it takes to convert stocks into a saleable product and hence back into cash may vary from a year or more for, say, a shipbuilder, to days or even hours for a food retailer.

Besides process time, stock levels will depend on the size of product range manufactured or sold.

It would benefit a business manufacturing a range of 100 different products to standardise the components used within those products so far as is compatible with design and marketing parameters. Even so, that business will almost certainly carry a larger range of materials in stock than one manufacturing just one product.

So there are no hard and fast rules about how much stock to carry. It is a matter of business strategy.

What is important from the point of view of controlling cash flow is that some form of stock control policy is in place. That policy should embrace a number of areas.

Product range

Marketing strategy may depend on manufacturing or offering for sale a comprehensive range of products. But every additional product will almost certainly increase stock levels. There is a need therefore to recognise that there is a level of expected sales or sales below which it is not viable to add or to continue to stock particular items.

Stock control policy should include setting and reviewing such levels.

Product design

In manufacturing businesses, product design will have a signifi cant impact on stock levels. Stock control policy should include consideration of the practicality of using standard components. In instances where design requirements mean stocking non-standard items it might be advisable to consider buying in rather than making components – this way the stock problem is passed on to the sub-contractor.

Buying policy

Prices for raw materials and finished goods may vary from time to time depending on market conditions. It is also true that it may be more economical to buy in quantity despite the possibility of holding stocks for longer than average.

And there is availability to be considered. Will an essential stock item suddenly become scarce or unavailable? Will deliveries become erratic for some reason or another?

Buffer stock levels

Bringing the three areas above together, the stock control policy depends on there being a formal process for deciding whether or not a particular line should be stocked and in what quantities. In other words, there should be a minimum order level and buffer stock level set for each item.

The buffer stock level will reflect expected usage, with a margin for error, during the likely delivery period. The minimum order level will reflect the current price and quantity discount level and expected future price movements. Both buffer stock levels (the point at which the reordering process is triggered) and minimum order levels should be reviewed frequently.

Internal control

Internal control was covered in Chapter 5, 'Preventing leaks'. It is an important element in stock control since stocks are particularly vulnerable to waste, misuse and loss.

Production control

Likewise, controls should be in place to monitor and minimise material wastage during the production process. This may mean setting a standard for each item produced so that actual material usage can be compared with the standard and any variance investigated.

Costing

A standard costing system can be used to keep tabs on material usage and how this has varied from the expected level. Wastage in usage can be identified and controlled.

Redundant stock

Stock levels can be easily overstated by the inclusion of out-of-date or redundant stock. It is important not to fool yourself into thinking stock is worth more than it is, and to bite the bullet by writing down values to realistic levels.

There is no point holding stock that is unlikely to be used, however much it has fallen in value. By far the best course is to sell it off for the best offer, so turning it into cash.

Monitoring

Above all, stock levels should be monitored. Is the overall value falling or rising? If it is rising – and hence eating up cash resources – is there a sound business reason? If not something should be done about reducing the amount held so as to improve the cash position.

8. Emergency moves

Effectively run businesses will operate near the edge by design. Not so well-managed concerns may often teeter towards the edge by accident. In both cases there will be times when fast action is needed to avoid plunging into the abyss.

Businesses that cannot pay their bills as they fall due are technically insolvent. Should total liabilities to outsiders exceed total assets, the business is definitely on the slippery slope.

All is not necessarily lost. Many businesses are insolvent from time to time, especially in the early days, but stay afloat to sail on into more favourable winds.

Even so, directors of companies should be extremely careful when faced with cash flow difficulties since to trade on when the company is insolvent could easily result in personal liability for the debts of the company and possible disqualification from acting as a director of another company.

Those in control of businesses in danger of collapse should be particularly careful not to accept credit when there is no reasonable prospect of payment and not to give anyone, or any one group of creditors, preferential treatment. Money owed to themselves, relatives or to others to whom personal guarantees have been given should not be settled in advance of other creditors with equal claims. Such action could amount to a fraudulent preference.

What follows are suggestions for the type of emergency measures that can be used to overcome a short-term cash flow hiatus – action that may give time for normal service to be resumed or for needed long-term changes to be implemented.

Assess the situation

Draw up a schedule of expected receipts and necessary payments. Convert this into a short-term cash flow statement showing expected net cash movements on at least a weekly interval frequency. Discover how much the shortfall will be and how long it is likely to last.

Ban buying

Put restrictions on all ordering whether of goods for resale, raw materials or other supplies. Review and reduce authorisation limits.

Borrow from the owners

Ask the owner or owners if he, she or they can put more money into the business by way of a loan or increased capital. Can they cut or waive any regular drawings from the business? Can they offer additional security to the bank or provide a loan guarantee? Can they do without use of a company car so that it can be sold off?

Chase your debtors

See if it is possible to speed up the issue of sales invoices. Make sure chasing procedures are operating properly. Consider reducing the timescale for chasing and strengthening appeals and warning letters. Identify overdue accounts where legal action could be commenced. Make sure all outstanding queries are answered and, if necessary, agree to give credits for disputed items so that there can be no excuses for withholding payment.

Consider the credit card

If you have a credit card, can this be used to cover some payments and thereby gain additional, if expensive, credit?

Cut production

Damaging to the longer-term prospects of the business, cutting production may reduce wage costs in the short term.

Direct debits

Consider cancelling all direct debits and standing orders. You will probably have to pay most eventually but it will take time for a request for payment to reach you and for a cheque to go through.

Don't panic

If the business is basically sound and you can demonstrate that it has a good future, your chances of survival are good. In an insolvency everybody loses out so there will be plenty of people on your side.

Explain the situation

Don't leave staff who don't know what is going on to deal with irate suppliers chasing payment. Make sure employees know what to say, that they do not give empty promises and, if necessary, can give a firm date for payment.

Factoring

It may take a little time to implement, but factoring – borrowing against outstanding debtors – will release cash, although at a price. But if you are in hock to the bank there will probably already be a charge on debtors, so bank permission is required.

Get advice

If you are unsure of your legal position, or need help on obtaining finance, get advice from a professional.

Hold a sale

If a retailer, announce a sale of stock at reduced prices. It may reduce profit margins but it should help cash flow. Extending opening hours may also help, provided this does not push up wages by more than the extra cash coming in.

Illegal trading

Don't. If you have no prospect of paying creditors as they fall due, you must not incur new debts. If in doubt get advice from a professional.

Invoice discounting

If there are particularly large sales invoices outstanding, consider borrowing against these from an invoice discounter.

Jump on expenses

Issue instructions for business expenses to be kept to a minimum, introduce tougher authorisation procedures, suspend petty-cash replenishment.

Kill recruitment

Put a hold on all new recruitment. You may need more staff in the long run but right now recruitment will cost money and tie up valuable management time in interviews. And employing more staff will only increase the wages bill.

Look for new capital

Are there people who might like to become shareholders or partners? What about senior employees? Is there one or more you could invite to take a stake in the business?

Manufacturing changes

If a manufacturer, review length of run required for each product line. Consider making some items to order only. Can stocks of finished goods be run down? Can any be returned to the supplier or sold off?

New work

Is there work that can be undertaken, even if less profitable than usual, that would yield immediate payments?

Payment on account

If any new and major contracts are in progress or about to begin, ask for payment on account.

Pensions and insurance

If you are the owner and have a pension scheme, can it be used to get funds into the business? Is there a life-assurance policy that can be surrendered for cash? Is there a surplus in the company pension scheme that can be put back into the company? Can payments for insurance and pension schemes be suspended temporarily? If not, are there insurances or personal pension schemes that can be cancelled or frozen?

Post-date cheques

Consider issuing post-dated cheques with an explanation of current circumstances.

Put off avoidable expenditure

Delay capital spending plans, advertising or other expenditure whose timing is not crucial to immediate survival.

Quicken up bankings

Make sure all cheques are banked as soon as received. For larger cheques consider paying out for express clearance.

Revise terms of trade

Consider revising terms of trade so that credit periods are reduced. Introduce a discount for prompt payment of bills (but see pages 67–8).

Run down stocks

Wherever possible, adapt items in stock for use rather than buy in new supplies.

Sale and lease back

Does the business own outright a building or substantial piece of plant or equipment or a vehicle? If so, it may be possible to arrange for a finance company to buy the item and lease it back to the business.

See the bank manager

If the problem is short term and you can show it to be that – with budgets and cash flow statements – the bank manager is likely to be understanding. How understanding will depend upon the amount and the time span involved. But if you need an increased overdraft facility, can justify the need, give assurances on risk, show how the interest can be met and repayment is possible, then the facility is likely to be granted.

Sell something

Is there a company car, little-used piece of machinery or other item that can be sold quickly?

Stop paying bills

An obvious and immediate, possibly forced, means of helping cash flow is to hold back on payments. Most businesses can get away with delaying payments by a few days, even weeks, on odd occasions. If longer is needed, talk to creditors. Tell them your problem and how you will overcome it. Suggest a revised schedule of payment which you can meet. Most would prefer some payment rather than none at all and the possible loss of a customer.

Target larger customers

If you have one or a number of larger customers with money due or nearly due, target them for a call. If necessary tell them something about your circumstances, ask for payment on account or as soon as possible.

Undertake a review

Look at the profitability of the business. Review budgets and compare with actual results. Identify costs that have exceeded expectations and areas for possible savings. Review number and profitability of product lines. Consider cutting out less profitable lines.

Value added tax

Make sure all possible claims have been included for bad debts. If not include on next return. Consider whether the current basis of assessment is most favourable to the business and whether a change is possible.

Value the business

What assets can be offered as additional security against a loan? Consider having buildings and other assets revalued if this is likely to demonstrate a surplus that will impress the bank or other existing or potential providers of finance.

Wage costs

Ban overtime. Are there casual workers that can be laid off? If not, are there other ways wage costs can be reduced by lay-offs or redundancies, without incurring higher severance costs?

Zero rated

Businesses whose sales are zero rated for VAT purposes can expect refunds of VAT. They should therefore make sure VAT returns are submitted as promptly as possible.

9. Tide tables

The first rule of navigation is to know your starting position. If you know where you are, you can plot a course. If you don't, no amount of reckoning can guarantee a safe destination.

The successful captain plots a safe course and then checks continually on how market pressures and the ebb and flow of the cash tide have conspired to push his or her vessel one way or another. And the captain goes on to adjust the helm accordingly. Positional checks are not the bearings of the seafarer but the comparisons, ratios and reconciliations of the business person.

Budgets, including, of course, cash flow statements, have plotted the expected course and destination. Comparisons between budgets and actual results reveal leeway and drift. Ratios and reconciliations provide the landmarks and buoys.

Budgets, essential for planning, are also invaluable for checking progress and correcting the inevitable unexpected. They provide the basis for regular comparisons between what was thought likely and what has in fact occurred.

Every business should make such comparisons from time to time. The larger and the more sophisticated the business, the more frequent and detailed the comparison should be. But certain key items such as sales revenue, major costs, operating profit and cash position should always be included.

If an item is important enough to command a line in the budgets, it is usually important enough to do the same in management accounts – and therefore deserves attention.

If the business is large enough to have a separate accounting and finance function, its manager should be in a position to home in on a comparison of more detailed cash flow factors. The idea is to identify and understand variations from budget. And the up-shot may be corrective action or a revision of future plans, with all the cash and other consequences that will be involved.

Being ahead of the budget deserves just as much attention as being behind. Unplanned expansion can outstrip financial resources and destroy cash flow projections.

Part of knowing where you are involves making what checks are possible to verify that management accounting information is correct and that you are not losing opportunities by anticipating events too far in advance. In the cash area, this means reconciling the balance that the books show you have in the bank with that which bank statements show.

There will usually be a difference between the two, simply because of the time it takes for cheques you send others to be banked and charged against your account, and because of the time it takes cheques you have banked to be credited to your account. Other reasons for differences could be forgotten standing orders or direct debits, payments transferred direct to your account, bank charges, even your own or bank errors.

The important thing is that if cash is to be controlled and the most made of your bank-account resource, you need to know where you are. This means making regular and frequent reconciliations.

Another reconciliation which is undertaken by companies annually is to prepare a 'statement of application and sources of funds', often more simply known as a 'funds flow' statement. This reconciles the movement of cash with profit and loss account and balance sheet movements.

Ratios and percentages can provide useful markers that either help interpretation of budget comparisons or stand as beacons in their own right.

Everybody uses ratios. Speed – miles per hour – consumption – miles per gallon or cigarettes per day – are ratios often heard in everyday conversation.

'I smoked 100 cigarettes' may be interesting. 'I smoked 100 cigarettes last year', is more meaningful information. By putting two facts together, interpretation is possible.

The same applies to financial figures. 'Debts outstanding of £1m' is a statement of fact with no context or relevance. 'Debts outstanding of £1m equal one day's sales' puts a new complexion on the statement. The ratio of debts to sales is useful.

As with all financial information, there is no point in calculating ratios unless they are relevant and useful. Calculating every figure possible would be a waste of energy, and probably confusing into the bargain. But key ratios selected as especially pertinent to the business can be helpful.

Below are some suggestions for ratios that could be useful and help in understanding and controlling a business and, in particular, its cash flow.

Balance sheet structure

Gearing

Gearing expresses to what extent a business relies on borrowings (rather than equity capital or retained profits) to finance its capital needs. When interest rates are lower than expected rates of return from the business, then high gearing will help to push up profits. But high gearing always involves an element of risk since highly geared businesses are vulnerable to rising interest rates or falling trading profits, or both. Cash flow will suffer because interest and scheduled repayments cannot easily be avoided.

There are a number of ratios that can be calculated to indicate gearing or its effect.

Loan capital as a percentage of total capital is the simplest. Clearly this figure is unlikely to fluctuate considerably over the short term.

Interest payments as a percentage of operating profits (or sales, or pre-tax profits) brings in both reliance on borrowings and the effect of interest rates. A rising figure could spell danger.

Liquidity

As was said earlier (Figure 1.4), fixed assets should, as a general rule, be financed out of long-term finance. This in turn must mean that current assets will not be less than current liabilities. If they are then the business could be in difficulty meeting its debts as they fall due. This could be so in any case if a large proportion of current assets are tied up in, say, raw material stocks, when it takes several months to complete the production cycle and several more to collect the cash from a sale.

For this reason current assets are sometimes divided between 'quick assets' (those assets such as cash and debtors which are already cash or can be turned into cash quickly), and other current assets.

All these ideas can be wrapped up into a few simple ratios.

Current assets divided by current liabilities gives an overall indication of structure – and of liquidity. A figure of 1 or more means that current assets outstrip current liabilities and must also mean that fixed assets are more than covered by long-term finance.

A figure of less than 1 could spell trouble.

The 'quick ratio' (cash, debtors and marketable securities divided by current liabilities) is a more stringent test. If the figure is 1 or above the business is well covered.

Working capital control

Working capital comprises current assets less current liabilities.

As explained above, financial stability usually entails having an excess of assets over liabilities – and therefore a plus figure for working capital. But there is only so much of a good thing.

Unless net current assets represent money stashed away in a revenue-earning account or invested in securities that can be sold at the drop of a hat, then current assets represent dead money. In themselves they are not earning, they are there waiting to be used or turned into cash.

In other words, while financial stability requires working capital to be a positive figure in most cases, efficiency requires the excess to be as low as is decently possible. This means keeping control of stock and debtor levels and making the most of trade creditors.

Stock control

Ratios can be calculated to throw light on control of raw material stocks, of work in progress and of finished goods stocks – and on the overall stock position.

Raw material stocks divided by average daily material costs gives an indication of the number of days' worth of raw materials. The less tied up in raw materials – the fewer days' worth – the better, provided the figure is not too low to meet requirements within replenishment periods or shortages, there are no delivery problems and price rises are not expected.

Similarly, work in progress divided by average daily total production costs will give an indication of the number of days' worth of production in progress. Again, within limits, the fewer the number of days the tighter the control.

And the finished stock figure can be divided by average daily production costs or, if manufacture is not involved, average daily purchase costs, to give an indication of the number of days' worth of stock held.

The overall figure and, if desired, each element of stock, can be expressed in terms of days' sales.

On the one hand, stocks are valued at cost, not sales value, so there is a slight inconsistency in this approach – especially if mark-up varies considerably from range to range. But if production and sales levels are at variance – where, say, a business is making for stock because orders have fallen off – it could be more meaningful to relate stock levels to sales.

Some people prefer to express such ratios as 'number of times turned over in a year' results, achieved in this instance by dividing sales by stock and forgetting about the number-of-days element.

Credit control

Similar ratios can be calculated for debtors to indicate degree of credit control.

Debtors divided by average daily sales gives an indication of the average number of days' sales outstanding. The lower the answer, the better, since less money will be tied up.

Other ratios can throw light on why the figure is not lower. The number of overdue accounts – taken from the aged debtors list – as a percentage of total debtors will, when compared with previous results for the same ratio, show whether more or less customers are moving into this band. Bad debts as a percentage of sales will pinpoint bad-debt experience and show whether there has been a purge which has helped to make the overdue accounts percentage look better.

Overall efficiency

Over the life of a business the most important source of cash is trading. But it will only come if the business is efficient and trades profitably.

An indication of overall success in these areas is provided by the return on capital percentage – profit times 100 divided by capital employed – or net assets, which equal the same. Needless to say, the higher this figure the better.

In general terms, a good result can come from efficient use of assets and/or high profit margins – the last achieved through controlling costs in relation to selling prices.

The three key ratios, return on capital, asset usage (sales divided by assets) and profit margin (profits times 100 divided by sales) have a fixed mathematical relationship. Asset usage – the number of times assets are 'turned over' during the period – multiplied by the profit margin percentage will equal return on capital.

Delving further, asset usage can be analysed by dividing different categories of asset into sales – as in the stock turnover ratio mentioned above.

Dividing sales by fixed assets or different categories of fixed assets could be useful in indicating that they are being used efficiently. So there might be figures for number of times vehicles and, separately, plant, are turned over each year.

However, the results will be affected by the age of the assets concerned, since depreciation is written off book values each year. The way round this is to divide the original undepreciated cost figures into sales. Or, if preferred, another calculation could show the written-down value of each asset category as a percentage of the original cost. The lower the percentage, the more that has been written off and the older the average age of the assets included – not forgetting that different depreciation rates apply to different categories of asset.

Profit margin results can also be analysed further by relating each category of costs to sales.

The number of ratios and percentages that can be calculated is endless. They can mix physical and monetary figures. For example, employees per square foot could be a useful measure of office space usage, worker hours per £1,000 of production a useful measure of production efficiency.

In the cash control area, chasing letters sent per month or, say, cash banked this month as a percentage of sales invoiced in the month ending 30 days previously, might be helpful.

A few, carefully selected ratios of this type can, when compared over time, give early warning that cash flow predictions are somehow threatened.